An Illu

Covering 200 ye...

AN ILLUSTRATED CHRONICLE OF MY FAMILY

COVERING 200 YEARS

BY

WINSTON JONES

*Published by
Rhosygwalia Books*

Published in 2006 by
Rhosygwalia Books
Triolbrith, Rhos, Llangeler
Llandysul, Carms., SA44 5AE.

ISBN 0-9553343-0-6
978-0-9553343-0-6

Printed and bound in Wales by
Dinefwr Press Ltd.
Rawlings Road, Llandybie
Carmarthenshire, SA18 3YD

Dedicated to the memory
of my
father and mother

Acknowledgements

I wish to express my gratitude to the following people for allowing me to take photographs, for giving me certain information, and for their advice and encouragement:

Mr and Mrs Herbert, Pantymeillion
Chris and Paul Shadbolt, Gilfachwenisaf
Bill Hewitt, Gilfach
Richard MacCartney, Gellidywyll
Mrs Burford, Troedrhiw
Vicki Garna, The Post Office, Blaencelyn
Lea Jones, Tŷ Capel, Maenygroes
David Pritchard, Gwndwn
Mair Jones, Alma
Priscilla Jones, Maesyrawel
Gwynoro Jones, Llwydcoedisaf
Melfydd Jones, Cwmhyfryd
Geler Jones, Nantglas
Mrs M. A. Griffiths, Lluest
Dr Leslie Baker-Jones, Danygribin House
Mr and Mrs Robinson, Penrallt
Hilda Davies, Talar Wen
Janice Vasami, Manteg
Myra Davies, Y Ffawydd
Arthur Evans, Llandysul

Finally, I would like to thank my wife, Dr Gill Jones, for typing, proof-reading, and transferring this script to disc. I take full responsibility if there are any errors within this script.

CONTENTS

INTRODUCTION

I am very fortunate to have been blessed with a good memory for dates and certain things that are of interest to me. In fact, I have very often been asked by many people: 'Why don't you write things down? You remember every little detail – dates and other things.' It's probably because I have good hearing, as well as a good memory, that I remember the stories that my father and mother told me about the Triolbrith family going back three generations, and the stories of their friends and neighbours. My Uncle Dan (the author D. Parry Jones) also contributed very generously to my interest in local history, as well as family history. Later, I will include in this book some of the letters he sent to me. As well as my parents and Uncle Dan, my Great Uncle Sami (my grandfather's youngest brother, and who was also born at Triolbrith in 1883) provided me with many interesting stories. I used to spend a lot of time with him during the time that I was working in Rhyddgoedfawr, Newcastle Emlyn, for my Aunty Liz. At that time Great Uncle Sami had retired from farming, but used to come over to Rhyddgoedfawr to help with the harvest and other work, and often in the evening, I would go over to his cottage, sit in front of the fire, and listen to him telling stories of when he was young. To me, these people are the unsung heroes of the Welsh countryside. Quite unconsciously, they have instilled in us all a sense of belonging to something that is fundamentally invaluable – something to treasure and pass on. I have checked dates of births, marriages, and deaths from various family Bibles, church registers, and from headstones in different churchyards and cemeteries. Up to a certain time, however, the names of people's homes were not included in the church registers.

I have to write from memory because there is no-one left for me to talk to from the older generation, apart from one cousin to my mother, Marged Ann Griffiths. She answered many questions, and provided a rich source of information about Mother's side of the family. Of course, there is modern technology – the internet and so on – but I prefer to depend on my memory and the story-telling skills and recollections of my antecedents, to whom I am forever indebted. As well as a bit of the history of my father's family, who have lived here at Triolbrith for several generations, I am also including as much as I know of the history of my mother's family, some people as far afield as Patagonia and Canada.

I was speaking to one of my cousins last summer, and she asked me whether I could help her find a photograph of our grandparents. I informed her that I have quite a collection of family photos, and I gave her a photo of my grandparents. This gave rise to a considerable amount of interest among several of my grandparents' descendants, so – rather than keeping the photos locked up in a cupboard where no-one can see them – I will catalogue them and publish them. It is too easy to lose touch with whose photo is whose (the following photo illustrates this), so I will bring them out for an airing so that they can see the light of day.

Two ladies from my family album (identity unknown).

Thomas and Mary Jones, Triolbrith, and the entire family
– photograph taken at the farm about 1920.

I am also spurred on by the fact that at Triolbrith we nearly lost all our possessions in a fire last March. Were it not for Gill (my wife)'s shoulder pain at 4.30 a.m., and her getting up for a painkiller only to discover the chimney fire, we might have lost everything. The quick and professional response of the Llandysul fire brigade led to a satisfactory outcome. This incident has motivated me to share what I have got, for other people to enjoy.

Winston Jones

Chapter 1

TRIOLBRITH

I was born in the farm called Triolbrith, in the parish of Llangeler, Carmarthenshire, and I still live here today. I think I should begin by looking at the name of the farm, Triolbrith, and give a short account of the history of the place. Until about 1915 it was spelled Tryalbrith. In fact, in the OS map of 1906 'triol' was spelled that way, and so also were Tryalmawr, Blaentryale, and Tryalmaengwyn – but now they are all spelled the same way, with a 'Triol'. Many people have asked me the meaning of the word 'Triol'. Some say that it is because the farmlands of these farms are triangular in shape, others say that it means 'tair heol' (in English, 'three roads'), others say that 'Tryal' was the original name of the stream that starts under the farm yard in Blaentriole and runs down between Triolbrith and Triolmawr (however, this stream is not named on the OS map of 1906). The latter explanation has some credence because between Triolbrith and Gaerwenuchaf is another stream – named on the OS map as Nant Einon. Its source of origin lies beside a small, now ruined, cottage called Blaeneinon. It runs down past the farm Cwm-nanteinon before joining the unnamed stream to complete the triangle of land that is Triolbrith. It then runs down for about 300 yards to a small ruined cottage called Cwmllwyd, before joining the river Siedi (which originates above Blaensiedi). It seems, therefore, that the farms have been named according to their position in relation to the nearby streams. However, according to Professor Melfyn Richards of the University of Wales, Bangor, the word 'triol' refers to the 'tŷ un-nos' – the one-night house. Historically, to stake claim to a piece of land, a person had to build a house on a plot of common land in one night. The claimants would have to get all the materials that they needed, and all their friends ready to help. They would choose one night in November or December when the day was short and the night at its longest – hopefully with a full moon and a clear night so that there would be no clouds covering the moon. At dawn the following morning, when they had smoke coming out of the chimney, they would ask the local blacksmith to throw the axe in four directions from the new building. Wherever the axe landed, the piece of land enclosed would be pegged out as the boundaries for their plot, and according to Professor Richards that piece of land was called a 'triol'. Personally, I prefer to believe Professor Richards' explanation rather than the other theories about the 'tair heol', or the triangular piece of land.

As well as discussing the name of the farm, I should explain something about the landlord. Whoever lived and farmed here at Triolbrith would have to rent the farm from the Church Commissioners. The farm was ecclesiastical property within the provisions of the Welsh Church, and towards the second half of the eighteen hundreds was soon to be transferred to the Representative Body of the Church in Wales – by orders made by the *'Governors of Queen Anne's Bounty for the Augmentation of the Maintenance of the Poor clergy or the Welsh Commissioners'*. The rent at the time when my great grandfather took over the tenancy was £50 per annum, and the rent had to be paid to the incumbent of Llanddarog Church, Carmarthenshire. Therefore the incumbent had to act as the agent for the landlords. He had to come and inspect the farm from time to time to make sure it was farmed in accordance with good husbandry in order to comply with the agreement between landlord and tenant.

The Church Comissioners owned farms and land in several parishes in Carmarthenshire – namely, in the parishes of Abergwili, Conwil, St. Peter's, Newchurch, Llangunnock, Trelech, Merthyr, Llangeler, and Laugharne. Perhaps it is worth mentioning the names of some of the farms – for example:

- In the parish of Abergwili: Caeglas Towy, containing 14 acres, and Ystrad Issaf, 32 acres.

- In the parish of St Peter's: Pentremeurig, 34 acres, Morfa fields, Nantyrarian fields, and also two fields known as Parcydrissy and Parcypost adjoining the farm known as Parcydelyn.

- In the parish of Trelech: Rhosychain, 61 acres, Tyddynfari, 46 acres, and Glyngarthen, 89 acres.

- In other parishes: Cwmcastell, 31 acres, Llechllwyd, 69 acres, Langorsfach, 26 acres, Cwmnanteinon, 28 acres, Cilmarchau, 208 acres, Tynewydd, 52 acres, and Nantclawdduchaf, 204 acres.

In the Triolbrith agreement between the Church Commissioners and the farmer, it states:

Triolbrith: Situate in the Parish of Llangeler, containing 93 acres, 3 roods, 5 perches of good sound pasture and arable land, and the rent will be £50 per annum.

Triolbrith, around 1930.

THE BUILDINGS comprise a good Stone-built and Carnarvon slated Dwelling-house.

THE OUTBUILDINGS consist of a 3-Stall Stable, with loft over, Cowshed for 10 ties, Barn, Piggeries, Calves' Cots' Cart-house with loft above, Implement Shed (all stone built and in good repair).

One of the things that I must admire is the outstanding engineering skill of whoever designed the water system at the farm. There was always a good supply of water diverted from the stream above the road, coming down through the fields called Rhoswarfach, Parcmawr, Parcnewydd, Parc-danrhiw. The water then flowed into the pond where it was stored to give enough force to turn the water wheel which worked the barn threshing machine, and the grinding mill for the corn, and other things. The overflow that bypassed the pond came to the pistyll (spout) where the horses and cows were watered. From the pistyll, the water ran across the bottom of the farmyard, in through the 'tŷ bach' (outside toilet), and from there, back to the stream. There was a good clean water supply for drinking, cooking, and washing the dairy utensils, but it had to be carried up from the ffynnon (well), which is down by the stream in the bottom of Parc-gwairuchaf. Most of the time, this was a job for the youngest children.

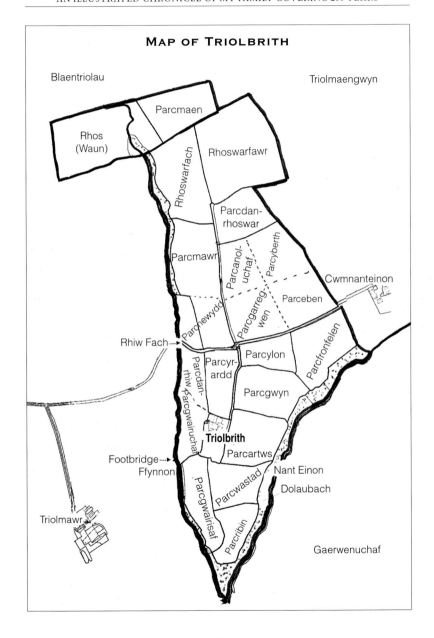

MAP OF TRIOLBRITH

Blaentriolau

Triolmaengwyn

Parcmaen

Rhos
(Waun)

Rhoswarfach

Rhoswarfawr

Parcdan-
rhoswar

Parcmawr

Parcanol-
uchaf

Parcyberth

Cwmnanteinon

Parcgarreg-
wen

Parceben

Parchewydd

Rhiw Fach

Parcfronfelen

Parcyr-
ardd

Parcylon

Parcdan-
rhiw

Parcgwairuchaf

Parcgwyn

Triolbrith

Footbridge
Ffynnon

Parcartws

Nant Einon

Parcgwairisaf

Parcwastad

Dolaubach

Triolmawr

Parcribin

Gaerwenuchaf

Chapter 2

THE EVANS FAMILY

The first family who lived in Triolbrith that I know anything about is the Evans family. The father of the family was a first cousin to my great great grandfather, Thomas Jones (who lived at Pantymeillion, Penboyr). There were four children in the Evans family, but the only one about whom I have heard anything is the eldest boy. He was somewhat restless, and felt very strongly that the new railway should not be cutting through the countryside. One evening, he went to the valley below Nantyrhebog – where the railway ran between Llanpumsaint and Pencader – and somehow managed to derail the train. Luckily no-one was injured. Someone must have seen him because, soon afterwards, he was arrested. I have been told that he was about 12 or 13 years old at the time. Subsequently, as punishment, he was sent to – what was called in those days – a 'Raget School', where he was severely punished. Today, our equivalent is the Young Offenders' Institution. All this was a great strain on his father, mother, and the other children. How long he remained in that school

I'm not very sure – although someone said about six years. During the time he was there he learned a trade and became a builder. When he was released, he came home to see his parents, but could not settle down – so he went off to America to work as a builder. He worked hard, and started his own building firm. That firm became very successful, building skyscrapers in Chicago. The firm is still in existence today, with a turnover of hundreds of thousands of dollars a year. Descendants of the Evans family have been back here from America a couple of times, to see his birthplace.

Soon after he left for America, sadly, his mother died, and is buried in the parish of Cynwil Elfet (now spelled Cynwyl Elfed). Afterwards, his father and the rest of his family moved to a farm called Glynmaenllwyd, and later to Nant-cwmrhys in the parish of Cynwil Elfet. The date by this time was 1867.

Chapter 3

THE EARLY DAYS
OF THE JONES FAMILY

The Jones family have been living at Triolbrith continually from 1867 until the present time – I am of the fourth generation to live here – before me, my father lived here, before him, my grandfather, and before him, my great grandfather, Benjamin Jones.

My great great grandfather, Thomas Jones, was the father of Benjamin, my great grandfather who moved to Triolbrith in 1867. Thomas was married to Sarah, and they lived at Pantymeillion, Penboyr.

Thomas was born in 1808 and died in 1896; Sarah was born in 1818, and died in 1895. It always amazes me when I think of their ages. Great great grandfather was born during the time of Abraham Lincoln, Napoleon the third, and William Gladstone, and my great grandfather, Benjamin, was born long before the civil war in America.

Thomas was a haulier by trade – he would travel long distances carrying goods with his team and wagon. The roads

Pantymeillion, as it is today.

at that time were poor, and night time was quite dangerous because of highway robbers. One place with a notorious reputation for highwaymen was Cware Bach on the Rhosgeler flats.

Thomas and Sarah Jones lived all their lives at Pantymeillion, Penboyr. They had eight children.

Benjamin the eldest was my great grandfather. He was born in 1842, and married Elizabeth Jones at Llangeler Parish Church on 22nd October, 1866. Elizabeth (b.1845) was the daughter of Thomas Jones, Penffosddu – now called Maesyrhaf. I know she had one sister, Marged, who later became Marged, Pencaerau Mawr, Blaencoed. She had a large family. Two of her boys emigrated to Canada. One returned, and the other stayed in Canada until he died. Elizabeth and Marged were first cousins (on their paternal side) to John, Triolmawr, and to Thomas, Cwmnant, who were brothers. Thomas died of blackthorn poisoning, and John's descendants farm at Triolmawr to this day.

My great great grandparents' second child was Sarah, and the third was Marged. Their fourth child was Mari, who was later the mother of Jams, Brynglas – the local carpenter referred to in 'Welsh Country Upbringing' by D. Parry Jones as 'Jim, the carpenter'. Their fifth child was called Enoch – he farmed at Glynrhodin, Maesllyn. Then came Beti (she became the second wife of 'Sam Lamb', and they both ran the Lamb Inn, Rhos), and after her came Hannah – she lived at Maengwyn, and was the mother of Hannah Sexton. There

23

was also John – I'm not sure where he came in the family. One interesting point about Hannah is that she walked thirty miles to Llandeilo to carry an orphaned baby back and bring it up as her own child. (The mother had been abandoned by her husband who had gone to America, and she had died in childbirth in the workhouse.) I am proud to be associated with such sympathetic people.

Thomas and Sarah Jones are both buried in the churchyard of Penboyr church. It is of interest to the family history that Thomas Jones' son, John, was buried the same day as his father – 13th December, 1876. He was 22 years old.

The Parish Church of Santllawddog, Penboyr.

Chapter 4

MY PATERNAL
GREAT GRANDPARENTS
AND THEIR FAMILY

Benjamin and Elizabeth, my great grandparents, came to
Triolbrith in 1867 – soon after they got married – so they
were the first 'Joneses' to live here. They had nine children –
six boys, and three girls.

The eldest was Thomas, my grandfather, born in 1867.
After he left school, he went to work for Thomas Williams,
Rhydfach, Llangeler, where he was introduced in a big way
to the world of horses, because Thomas Williams was a horse
trainer. My grandfather learned a great deal from this experience, and was in great demand in the neighbourhood for his
opinion on horses before they were bought or sold. After
about two years he moved to Penrallt Home Farm to work
for the Howell Jones family who lived in the mansion. It was
here that he met my grandmother who was also in service at
Penrallt. I will recount what I know of their story in the next
chapter.

He died in 1951, aged 84. I quote a few sentences from *The Carmarthen Journal* written by someone who knew him and the family well:

> *He was a well known and respected farmer and a prominent figure. The motto of the hearth at Triolbrith was genuine welcome and open kindness. He was a loyal churchman and a fine example of a countryman who walked naturally and neighbourly from day to day.*

I personally remember the crowds in his funeral, despite my being very young. I also remember eight clergymen coming to meet the body at the church gate. I feel proud to think that the country people felt that he and grandmother deserved such a tribute.

The second child was John. He married a girl from Caercadw, Henllan, and farmed at first in Penfedw, Brongest, before moving to Gwernant. Later, he moved to Beili, Llandygwydd, and stayed there until he retired. He had a large family of boys and girls. His descendants still farm at Beili.

The third child was Ben, who went off to the coal mining valleys of the Rhondda, where he worked and qualified as a saddler. He soon opened his own saddler's shop at 96 Dunraven Street, Tonypandy.

At that time, saddlery was a very important trade in the coal mining areas, as horses played such an important role underground, pulling the coal wagons. Ben became very

The Saddler's Shop, Tonypandy.

prosperous, and eventually bought Beili Farm, Llandygwydd, where he extended the house, designed and planted ornamental gardens, and gave the impression of affluence and superiority.

The fourth child was Rachel. She married Evan Simon Jones of Cefnmaesbach, and they had two daughters – Elizabeth and Gwyneth. Elizabeth farmed with her husband, Arthur, in Parcytrap, Newcastle Emlyn.

The fifth child was David. He married Ann who came from The Mill, Cenarth, and they farmed at Pengraig, Cenarth. After he retired, he lived at 'The White Hart', Cenarth, where his daughter, Bethan, managed the pub.

Once when I called to see him at The White Hart, he told me that he had also worked, at one time, at Penrallt home farm. His other daughter, Sarah, married, then she and her husband farmed in Pengraig, where the family still farms to this day. David and Ann also had one son, Ben, who married Maggie, and farmed at Penwernbica, Cenarth. Uncle Sami told me that when he and David were working at home in Gellidywyll, whenever the foxhounds came to the district, Sami and David would immediately saddle up and ride with them. In fact all the boys were keen horsemen, and their teams were well known in the convoys that travelled annually to the lime kilns.

The sixth child was Elizabeth. She married David Davies, who was in the milk trade at Llwynypia (Rhondda). She met him when she was helping her brother, in the shop in Tonypandy. The couple settled in the Rhondda, and had two children – a boy and a girl. The son joined the RAF during World War II, and was killed in a 'plane crash. The daughter, Bethan, became a nurse, married, and lived abroad for many years.

The seventh child was James who joined the Army, much to the disgust of his parents (according to Uncle Dan, 'A Welsh Country Upbringing') because they had intended him for the ministry:

. . . his joining the army had shocked and disgraced them all. He was the 'prodigal son' and his existence was hardly ever referred

to. When he did write home, it was to his younger sister, and if the family ever had any message for him, it was conveyed through her, as through a third person. Direct communication had been severed.

He served in the Royal Engineers in the Sudan. He was also in the Boer War in South Africa and, as well, served in India, and also in Egypt, attached to the Camel Corps. In his letters to Uncle Dan, he spoke of the Bedouin tribes in the desert. Apparently, the Bedouins resented the presence of the British Army, and the mothers would do all they could to prevent their sons joining up.

After James was invalided out of the Army – as a result of contracting enteric fever in Egypt – all was forgiven, and his family overcame their shame. He eventually retired and tried to settle down in Cenarth. However, he became increasingly restless. At every opportunity, he would buy a newspaper in Newcastle Emlyn, and would predict that there would be a war before long, which would be a World War. There would be machines and tanks. He was right. In 1914, the war started. He volunteered and joined up. He was sent to France, where he was killed in 1914. He is buried in France, but his name is on the family gravestone in Penboyr churchyard.

The eighth child was Samuel – Sami. He was born in 1883, died in 1962, and is buried at Gelli cemetery. I mentioned earlier that Great Uncle Sami contributed a great deal to my knowledge of our family history.

Sami, photo taken at Triolbrith, 1954.

When I was working at Rhyddgoedfawr, in 1955 and 1956, sometimes – in the evening – I would jump on my bike and freewheel down the road towards Newcastle Emlyn. Just before I came to 'the creamery' I would turn left up a lane towards Cwm. About 100 yards further, I would leave my bike leaning against a tree, and start climbing a steep path through the woods. At the top, I would cross one of Penlôn fields before reaching Sami's cottage – Pengraigyreithin. It was quite remote, but there was a lane (or it was more of a track) from the road between Newcastle Emlyn and Penbuarth. Finally, I would reach the cottage, and he would hear my boots on the cobbles, and would shout 'Who is it?' or 'Who's there?' in a loud voice, as he came out of the house or from the garden. If it was summertime, he would show me the garden before going into the house, where he would sit on his very old wooden armchair and talk about his life, the family, and the 'old days'.

There was one very sad chapter in Sami's life. His wife, Sarah Jane (who came from Penralltgillo), died in childbirth, aged 35. They had three children – Jenny (b.1906), Ben (b.1908), and David, born in 1917 when his mother died. David was brought up by Sami's sister, Rachel. In retrospect, I realise that this was an episode in his life that he deliberately blanked out as much as possible.

Well – back to the story-telling. He would gaze into the fire and puff away at his pipe. He loved to talk about his young days at Triolbrith and Gilfachwen Isaf and Gellidywyll.

Gilfachwen Isaf, as it is today.

He would always say things such as 'When I was in Penralltgillo', or 'When I was in Beili', because he farmed in Beili for three or four years – but he didn't get on well with his brother, Ben, who owned Beili. One day, one of Sami's cows ate from one of Ben's ornamental trees and died, because (according to the vet) the foliage was poisonous. So, Sami got the saw and the axe out, and cut down all the poisonous trees. When Ben found out, he immediately gave Sami notice to quit, on the grounds of negligence and poor husbandry. It all became very unpleasant, and ended up in the High Court, where the judge ruled in favour of Sami, because

Ben had behaved so unreasonably towards his brother. Then Sami decided to take over the tenancy of Penbuarth, Newcastle Emlyn, which was on the Cawdor Estate at that time. He stayed there until he retired in 1950, when Penbuarth was taken over by his nephew James and his family, and the same family remains there today. Remembering all that Sami told me, I feel that I was very privileged to have spent so much time with him. One thing I regret is that I did not have a tape recorder with me.

A few years later, when I was working at home with my parents, I visited Sami one evening. During the course of the conversation, he happened to mention that, when he was farming at Penbuarth, he and all the other tenants had had an invitation to go to Golden Grove, to see where Lord Cawdor lived. For some reason or other Sami hadn't gone, and had regretted it ever since. Well – I told him that my brother, Gwynoro, was Head Cowman at the College Farm in Golden Grove, and that I could go and see the place whenever I wanted. I told Sami that I would take him there if he wished. He jumped at the chance, and the following Sunday I picked him up, and off we went for the day. After we had had dinner with Gwynoro and Rita, we were shown all around the farm and the mansion. After tea, we came back here to Triolbrith for milking, then after supper I took him home. He said he had had a day to remember, and had fulfilled one of his wishes. I now realise that the time I spent with Sami has been invaluable, because of his positive attitude to everything that really mattered, and I think that a lot of this has 'rubbed off' on me.

The ninth child was Mary. She never married, and stayed with her mother until her mother died, then she moved to Aberarad, near Newcastle Emlyn. She is buried at Penboyr with her parents.

Of the nine children in this chapter, I only attended the funerals of four of them – Thomas, David, Sami, and Mary.

All of these children were born at Triolbrith, but when Thomas, my grandfather, got married, my great grandparents (and all the other children) moved to Gilfachwenisaf, Llandysul. How long they remained there I'm not sure, but they moved again to Gilfach, Llangeler.

Gilfach, as it is today.

Gellidywyll, Cenarth, as it is today.

Again, I'm not sure how long they lived there before moving again to Gellidywyll, Cenarth.

By this time, several of the children had got married and left home.

Benjamin, my great grandfather, died at Gellidywyll in 1905, and is buried at Penboyr. I remember Sami telling me that during his father's funeral, when the cortège came through Newcastle Emlyn, someone counted 140 traps and ponies following the hearse as they made their way up to Penboyr. My great grandfather must have been a very popular and well respected man, who had touched many people's lives in one way or another.

His wife, my great grandmother, followed him to Penboyr churchyard in 1928, so that was another milestone reached in the Jones' history.

Chapter 5

My Paternal Grandparents, Thomas and Mary Jones, and their Family

My Paternal Grandparents.

I have already explained who my grandfather was. My grandmother was the daughter of Daniel and Mary Evans of Troed-y-rhiw, Newquay.

Troed-y-Rhiw as it is today.

Daniel was a ship's carpenter. Ships were built in those days in many ports around the coast of Wales, built by local men for local men. Daniel and Mary had nine children.

The eldest was Sarah (b.1859, d.1933). She married Owen, a stonemason, and they had four children: Tom, Nellie, Mary (who farmed at Bola'r Fron, near Mwnt) and Danny (a ship's engineer, who was lost at sea during the First World War).

Elizabeth was their second child (b.1860, d.1956). She married David Williams, of Hengell Farm. He was a sailor, and rose to become a Captain. They had five boys. The youngest died at the age of fifteen. The other four went to sea. The eldest was Captain David Lewis, and his brother, Danny, became a pilot in the port of Swansea. The other two boys lost their lives at sea during the First World War. Their names are on the family gravestone at Maenygroes.

Henry (b.1862, d.1930) was the third child. He became a blacksmith. He had no family.

The fourth child was Mary, my grandmother (b.1864, d.1945). She is buried at St James' Church, Rhos. She left home early to live with some relatives at a farm called Cefen Ceilog, near Llangrannog, where she was never allowed to go to school. She learned to read and write in Sunday School, and was brought up a Congregationalist, but when she married, she joined the Church in Wales with my grandfather. She remained a loyal churchwoman for the rest of her life. When she died, Grandfather was unable to go to the funeral because he couldn't walk due to paralysis of the legs. When her body was carried out of the house, he cried after her 'Ffarwél, Mari Annwyl' (Farewell, my dear Mary). That was how they parted after 56 years together. In the *Carmarthen Journal, 11th January, 1946*, it was reported that her death took place on Christmas Eve, at the age of 82. The funeral took place the following Saturday, at St James' Church. The officiating clergy were: at the house, Revs. Richards, Troed-yraur, Talog Davies, Nantcwnlle, and Llewellyn Davies, Curate, and at the church and graveside, Revs. Owen Davies,

Tremain, D. Griffiths, Abergwili, Evans Davies, Llanllwch, Hywel Davies, Tonypandy, and D. Evans, Penboyr. Also present were the Rev. Henry Jones and the Rev. Derfel Rees, Minister of Siloh.

There were four younger children. The eldest was Rachel (b.1865, d.1866 of a brain fever), and next was Ben (b.1868, d.1928), buried at Rakeland Cemetery, Wallasey. One of Ben's sons was lost at sea off the coast of Newfoundland. Then came Tom (b.1869, d.1937). He had a son, Parry, and seven daughters – Mary, Myfanwy, Constance, Binki, Blodwen, and Betty. Binki was the only one to graduate – she took a degree in Zoology. She lived in Liverpool. After Tom came David, who settled in Australia, and died in 1928. Finally, there was Margaret (b.1877, d.1880).

Their mother (my great grandmother), Mary, Troedrhiw, was the daughter of Thomas and Sarah Parry of Y Blaen, Newquay, who are both buried at Maenygroes. Thomas was the son of Henry (b.1785, d.1858) and Rachel Parry (b.1784, d.1866) of Tir Pentref, Newquay. They were my great great great grandparents, and are both buried at Maenygroes, Newquay. Henry Parry was a descendant of Henry VIIth. At that time it was customary for the son to have the same name as his father, but they prefixed the son's name with 'ap' (son of). Gradually, the name 'ap Harry' became 'Parry' – which is how this surname originated. There is another piece of history – in fact more of a legend – that I would like to mention here, because it relates to Henry Parry. This event is supposed to have happened by the castle in Newcastle Emlyn, and the story was well-known locally. I would like to quote in full from one of my Uncle Dan's letters:

On one particular fair day when the town was thronged with people a fierce 'winged viper' breathing forth fire and smoke alighted on the castle walls and settled down to sleep. Its appearance wrought consternation and wild terror in the bosoms of all, but after the first spasms of fear had subsided a few brave spirits got together to see how they could get rid of it. There was a sailor present whom they consulted about the matter. The plan he suggested was to shoot it, and that the man who was to undertake this dangerous task should wade into the river Teifi (which nearly surrounds the castle) to a point of vantage above the castle, take with him a big red cloak, shoot the creature in a vulnerable part, i.e. in the underparts, and that would be easy as the wall was a considerable height above the river. After shooting it, he was to dive immediately under the water and let the red cloak float down on the surface of the river. That was the plan which was carried out to the letter, and it proved successful. The dragon, violently startled from its sleep, caught sight of the red cloak and, believing it to have something to do with the attempt on his life, fell upon it in its rage and tore it to shreds while his true assailant made quietly for the bank of the river. Soon the reptile turned on its back and floated down the river, poisoning everything in the river with the loathsome venom that poured from its wound. Now comes, for our family, the important and interesting fact – that sailor who planned the attack and carried it out was Henry Parry's brother.

I will now return to my grandparents, Thomas and Mary Jones. I have already mentioned how they met. As I said, sometime around 1886, grandmother was in service in Penrallt Mansion with the Howell-Jones family, and grandfather was simultaneously working there at the home farm.

I have been told that when Mary (Grandmother) had some free time – not very often I would imagine – she would go home to see her parents in Newquay which was about twelve miles away. Then Thomas (Grandfather) would go to Newquay to see her on a Saturday evening, after finishing work.

Penrallt Mansion.
(Photograph courtesy of Dr Leslie Baker-Jones).

41

Penrallt Home Farm.
(Photograph courtesy of Mr and Mrs Robinson).

He would walk and run most of the twelve miles, except when a pony and trap happened to catch up with him. Then he would hitch a lift for part of the way – and when the trap turned off on some other road, he would jump off, and walk again. Probably, another trap or carriage would catch him up again, and he would hitch another lift for some distance. He was on his way to see his girl-friend, and his heart must have been light, and he would have had a spring in his step.

They married on 14th of November, 1889, and took over the farm here, at Triolbrith where they stayed until they retired (great grandparents and the rest of the family moved from Triolbrith at this time to Gilfachwen Isaf, as I mentioned earlier).

They had ten children. The eldest was Ben, born in 1890.

Uncle Ben.

After leaving school, Ben left home and went to Tony-pandy in the Rhondda to gain an apprenticeship in saddlery with his uncle – also a Ben. He married a girl called Jeanie, and they had three boys – Beni, Davey, and Colin. Sadly, Uncle Ben died in 1934, aged 44, and he is buried in Trealaw cemetery.

Next came Daniel (b.1891, d.1981). After finishing school in Capel Mair, he attended the Grammar School in Pencader before going on to study at St David's Theological College, Lampeter.

The school at Capel Mair, where all the children had their early education (now used as a church hall).

St David's College, Lampeter.

44

Three years later, he was ordained at St Mary's Church, Abergavenny, by Bishop Hughes of Llandaff. He told me that one of the things he would have liked was to have his parents present at his ordination – their cup would have been full. But it coincided with a busy time at the farm, and they lived so far away. Uncle Dan said that that joy had been denied to them, as well as to himself.

Uncle Dan.

Uncle Dan and Aunty Gladys.

46

His first parish was in Pontypridd, and he was curate at St Catherine's, where the vicar was the Rev. Watkins-Edwards. From there, he moved to St Thomas' Church, Stockport, in the diocese of Chester. It was a parish of about fourteen thousand people. At that time, most people worked in the cotton mills, and lived in the slums.

Uncle Dan married Gladys Murgatroyd – she was the organist in one of the churches where he was curate. They eventually – after moving a few times to different parishes – settled down in Llanelli Hill, Gilwern, Abergavenny. They had three children – Pam, Peggy, and Peter.

They stayed in Abergavenny until Uncle Dan retired. He became Rural Dean of Crickhowell in 1957, and was made a Canon of Brecon Cathedral in 1959. After his retirement, he lived at 18 Allt-yr-Yn Crescent, Newport, Monmouthshire.

This is the account that appeared in the newspaper, October 27th, 1961, on the occasion of Uncle Dan's retirement:

GILWERN RECTOR WILL BE MISSED BY ALL DENOMINATIONS

The church schoolroom at Gilwern was crowded last week when members of local churches and chapels met to make a presentation to Canon D. Parry-Jones, rector of Llanelly Parish Church, Gilwern, and Mrs Parry-Jones. The rector, who has retired, and his wife will live in Newport.

47

Mr Parry-Jones was rector of the parish from 1936, and was also rural dean of the Crickhowell district, Hon. Canon of Brecon Cathedral and sub-warden of the Diocesan Association of Lay Readers.

For 20 years he was president of the Clydach and District Bible Society. He was connected with numerous other organisations, and is the author of three books.

During the Second World War he was an active member of the Gilwern detachment of the Home Guard.

GOOD ADVICE

Mr Lance Jones, chairman of the presentation committee, called on the Rev. J. M. Evans, vicar of Llangenny parish, to preside at the ceremony. The vicar will be in charge of Llanelly Church, assisted by the rector's warden, Mrs S. Davies, until the new rector arrives.

Paying tribute to the retiring rector, Mr Evans spoke of his work on behalf of the church and deanery of Crickhowell, and added: "I am not unmindful of the good advice and help the rector gave me when I was a young curate at Brynmawr."

Making the presentation of a cheque to Canon Parry-Jones and a tea service (given by Mrs Hartson) to his wife, Mrs S. Davies also referred to the work the rector had carried out during his 26 years in the parish. She spoke, too, of the services given by Mrs Parry-Jones as enrolling member of the Mothers' Union, and presented her with a bouquet of flowers.

Expressing thanks, Canon Parry-Jones said: "I am deeply touched by this presentation, knowing it has been contributed to by parishioners of all religious denominations.

"I have been in the ministry for 47 years, but I regard my 26 years in this parish as the most impressive of all." He added, "I shall look on Gilwern almost as my home, having loved the people, the churches, the mountains, hills, vales, fields and lanes. I hope to visit you from time to time to recapture some of the joys of living here.

"When I came to this parish, it was in the grip of unemployment and consequent depression, and there was great suffering and bewilderment among the people.

"Then came the Second World War, bringing its own peculiar sufferings, hardships and restrictions. In the first half of my ministry here, the churches could do little beyond trying to carry on. Then came the Welfare State, the rise in wages, the abundance of work and the good times.

"But strangely enough, the depression did not affect our church and our worshipping habits, and all the places of worship were well attended. It is the coming of the affluent society that has changed this. So many now possess cars, and Sunday has largely become a day when father takes his family with him to the seaside or for a run in the country.

"War-time efforts introduced Sunday work, and it still continues in many places.

"You will give my successor, I know, the loyalty that you have always given to me, and to his family, the regard and the friendship that you have always shown to mine."

49

Sadly, about eight years after Uncle Dan retired, Aunty Gladys passed away suddenly on the way home after they had spent a day out together.

Uncle Dan remarried Kate in 1975. Unfortunately, she did not live very long after the marriage, and I never had the privilege of meeting her, because her health was failing.

I remember going to see the church in Gilwern, years after he died. I was talking to the caretaker of the churchyard, and he mentioned that there had been a storm in 1989, and some of the big yew trees in the churchyard had been blown down. When the trees were sawn up, chains were found that had grown into the wood – and they had ruined the chainsaws. No-one could understand what the chains were doing up there in the branches. I was able to enlighten the caretaker by telling him what Uncle Dan had told me previously – that during the big snow of 1947, Uncle Dan had organised some of his parishioners to bind some of the branches together, so that the weight of the snow did not cause the trees to split down the middle. The snow cleared eventually, but the chains were left in the trees, and between 1947 and 1989 they had grown into the wood. Uncle Dan only told me that a few years before he died.

Uncle Dan came here to Triolbrith as often as he could. He told me that there was a place – it didn't matter where the place was, whether an old lane, footpath, moor, or village, anywhere, perhaps in the middle of England or Wales – which would always be in someone's mind, especially if that person lived in a big town or city. He said that the place always in his mind was the view from the fields at Triolbrith – the part of Carmarthenshire facing the whole length of the river Teifi, and the part of Cardiganshire on the other side of the Teifi that does not face the sea. He said he thought of the place where he was born and bred, before the advent of the tractor. He remembered seeing the other farms from our top fields, and counting forty pairs of horses ploughing at the same time.

A typical scene at the time.

These memories released any tension for him, and gave him a feeling of being close to nature. He always wanted to know what was going on at the farm at the moment – as will be seen later, in his letters to me.

Ploughing at Triolbrith today.

It was this love of the countryside and his home that inspired him to write his first book, *Welsh Country Upbringing*. After that he wrote several books: *Welsh Country Characters, Welsh Legends, My Own Folk, Welsh Children's Games and Pastimes,* and *A Welsh Country Parson.* They are easy to read, and contain so much information about a way of life that has disappeared from this country for ever.

Uncle Dan would often 'phone me to see whether there was any news in the locality. In turn, I would keep him informed if there was anything to report in the neighbour-hood, as I knew how much it meant to him. When he wrote he frequently encouraged me to research and write about my mother's family, as he said they had such an interesting history, needing to be passed on. He also invariably mentioned the two churches – Capel Mair and St James' – places that were very dear to his heart. It reminds me of the story he told me about his christening in Capel Mair. Apparently, Grandfather took the four eldest children to be christened when they were quite old – between the ages of four and seven. Just before the service, the children escaped and ran away, and Grandfather and the other church members had to give chase and round them up.

Capel Mair Church.

Uncle Tomi.

The third child to be born to my grandparents was Thomas (b.1892, d.1961).

He married Mary Elen, and they farmed in Llwyn-Neuadd, Penboyr. They had four children – Leslie, Parry, John, and Gwyneth. After Tomi retired, they moved to Llwyndyris Mansion, Llechryd. They are both buried at St James' Church.

The fourth child to arrive was Johnnie (b.1893, d.1951). He married Sarah, and they lived at Garregwen, Rhydlewis, where he was a saddler.

54

Uncle Johnnie.

They had two children – Geler and Mair. Johnnie was buried on the same day as King George VIth. He and Sarah are both buried at St James'.

The next child to be born was Mary (b.1894, d.1961). During the Great War she served with the Red Cross, nursing the injured.

She married Johnnie of Tyhen. The couple didn't have a family. They farmed at Nantygwair and at Maesgwyn, Llansteffan, and are both buried at Saron, Llangeler.

Aunty Mary in nurse's uniform.

Haymaking at Maesgwyn, Llansteffan.

The sixth child was David (b.1897, d.1958). He became a saddler, and eventually took over the saddler's shop in Tonypandy. He married Olwen, but they didn't have a family. They are both buried in Trealaw cemetery.

Uncle Dai.

57

Aunty Sal.

The next child was Sarah (b.1898, d.1976). She married Theophilus Thomas Jones (Uncle The). They farmed at Blaenbowi, Capel Ifan, and had four children: Tegwedd, Hedydd, Gwenfydd, and Melfydd. The same family still farms at Blaenbowi.

Aunty Liz, Aunty Sal and Aunty Mary.

Then came Henry (Uncle Har), b.1899, d.1968.

Uncle Har.

After leaving school, he had an apprenticeship in the grocery business in Newcastle Emlyn before he was called up and was drafted into the Machine Gun Corps.

Henry in the Machine Gun Corps.

He served throughout the war, but was wounded. After coming out of the Army, he also became a saddler like three of his brothers before him, learning the trade up in Tonypandy with their uncle. He took charge of the branch at Llewellyn Street, Pentre. Later he started his own saddlery business at 7a, Park Street, Llanelli. Uncle Har married Agnes, and they continued to live in Llanelli for the rest of their lives. They didn't have a family. They were both cremated at Morriston Crematorium.

The ninth child to be born was James, my father (b.1900, d.1961).

Father, aged about 17, when he was working in Swansea.

I will write a great deal more about him later, in the following chapters.

The last child to be born was Lizzie (b.1906, d.1984).

She married David of Gilwen farm, Newcastle Emlyn. They farmed at Rhyddgoedfawr, Newcastle Emlyn, and had two children – Tom and Jean.

Aunty Liz.

62

Aunty Liz with Tom and Jean.

Uncle Dafi with Tom and Jean, penning the sheep, ready for washing at Rhyddgoedfawr.

63

The family are all buried at Holy Trinity Church, Newcastle Emlyn.

Thomas, my grandfather kept a record of births in his Family Bible.

Birth Register from the Family Bible of Thomas and Mary Jones, Triolbrith.

Of the ten children born to my grandparents, five of the boys served in the Army during the Great War, and, of course, Mary in the Red Cross. It was a miracle that they all came home safely. I remember my father saying that three of the brothers met in Bonn at the end of the war – they met purely by chance – none of them knew that the others were there.

One thing that is worth mentioning here is that, during the war, Grandfather applied to the War Office to allow one or two of the boys to stay at home to work on the farm. The reply he had from the chairman of the War Tribunal was that the farm was too small, and that all the boys would have to go to war. After they came home, two were wounded, so grandfather applied on their behalf for a War Disability Pension. The reply came back – from the same chairman – that one of the boys could have a pension, but that the farm was big enough to support the other one. It shows the power of the chairman of the War Tribunal, that he could change the rules to suit himself. However, the important thing to my grandparents was that all their boys returned home alive.

When the children were growing up at Triolbrith, the boys would go out at night to sleep in the loft above the horses – and this is probably true of children in all the other farms where there were large families. The same would apply to boys from the local villages if they were working on the farms. Only the parents and the girls would sleep in the house. At what age the Triolbrith boys started sleeping outside I am

Ben, Tommy, James, Dai, Johnnie, Har, and Dan.

not sure. They would always sleep above the horses in the stable because, if the night was cold, it was the warmest place to be. In the morning, they would get up, and go into the house for breakfast before going off to school – which was a long way to walk, whichever way they went. In winter, they would go down through the valley, where they would be sheltered by the trees. In the summer, they went along the road along to Bwlchyddwyrhos, and down to Bancyffordd – both routes were about three miles long.

Father told me that his parents had one goose who would only sit on her eggs in the 'cwtsh dan star' – the cupboard under the stairs. It seems she wouldn't sit anywhere else, but

66

as soon as they brought her in, she would sit on her eggs for three weeks until they hatched. Every time someone important called, such as the vicar, she would cackle and want to come out to stretch her legs for a walk. She would be back in less than five minutes demanding to be let back into her cupboard under the stairs.

Mary, Sal, and Liz.

Thomas and Mary Jones, Triolbrith.

Chapter 6

MY FATHER

My father was the youngest of all the boys. He, like all the other children, began his education at Capel Mair, but by the time he had finished at that school, Brynsaron School had been built, and – because it was a little closer – Father and one or two of the other children moved to Brynsaron. People referred to it as 'Yr Ysgol Newydd' (The New School) for a few years afterwards. The headmaster was Mr Jones, Tygwyn, and he was replaced after his retirement by another Mr Jones. The latter was still headmaster there when I started school – but by the time I left, the headmaster was Mr Davies, Woodlands.

After leaving school, Father left home to look for work in Swansea. It is surprising how many young people, even at that time, were leaving the countryside for the towns to seek work. Four older brothers had already left home to do their apprenticeships in the saddlery trade in the Rhondda valley. Well, Father found work in a grocery shop, Lipton's – there was a branch of Lipton's in every big town. When Father was first interviewed, the manager asked him where he came from, whether he had grown up on a farm, and, if so, whether he was used to horses. Father replied that when he was in school, his father would send him with one or two of the younger children down to Llandysul railway station with the young horses, so that the horses would get used to the noise of the trains, the smoke, and the hissing of the steam. This was because there was no railway near the farm, and when Grandfather went to Carmarthen or Newcastle Emlyn, the road would sometimes run parallel with the railway. If the horses were not used to the trains, they would have bolted in fright causing a bad accident.

Llandysul Railway Station, 1932.

When the manager of the shop heard this, he immediately gave my father a job. His first task every morning was to take a horse and cart – or a gambo – down to the docks to fetch the goods that had been unloaded off the ships to be sold in the shop. I remember Father telling me that the first morning he went down to the docks, he lost his way. He went up to a policeman somewhere in the middle of Swansea to ask the way. The policeman remarked that Father must be new here, and that the best thing he could do was to let the horse show him the way! And that is what he did. It is worth mentioning that Father was only fourteen, had only been to Carmarthen once, and now, here he was in Swansea, which was much larger and further away. We can only imagine the steel wheel-bands clattering over the cobbled streets, the clopping of the hooves, and the shouting of men on their way to and fro over the Swansea streets.

Father must have grown up very quickly – after nearly a year, he was promoted to work in the shop, behind the counter. He had to learn how to weigh out almost everything – tea, sugar, coffee, tobacco, and so on. He was working some nights until 10.30 p.m., but he had every Sunday off. Once a Sunday, he would go to church, and every Sunday evening, he would go down to Mumbles on the little train. I can't remember where he used to lodge, but one of the people who lodged with him was the curate of St Peter's Church, where Father used to worship. I remember when Father was dying, he wanted to see this man. We tried to trace him, but alas, it seemed he had disappeared. There is a possibility that he had died by this time, or had been killed in the Great War.

When Father was eighteen, he was called up to join the Army, and he joined the South Wales Borderers.

Father in the South Wales Borderers.

He had to report to Brecon and, on the day that he joined up, two of his friends from Capel Mair School joined up the same day – Jim (Shadog) and Jack (Peglars). The three of them served together throughout – in Belgium and Germany – until the end of the conflict. But, for my father, the war was not over. He was sent to Ireland because of the troubles there, where he was appalled at the poverty, the poor conditions in which people lived, and the primitive state of farming and farm implements. Of Germany, he was warm in his praise, much admiring the great rivers, ancient cities, and the hard working intelligent people. Here is a poem he wrote on the back of a postcard, on his way back from the war:

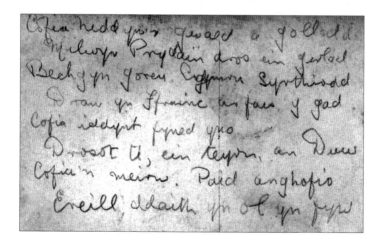

In it he laments his friends and others that fell in the war and asks us to remember them, but in the last two lines he also asks us not to forget others who came back alive.

After leaving the Army, my father came home to work on the farm with his parents. There was a shortage of timber after the war, so Grandfather – and some other farmers who had a large area of woodland – would cut down oak trees, and drag the trees up out of the woods near the streams. The following Spring they would have a timber sale, and it proved to be quite a profitable sideline, although it was very hard work.

My father spoke frequently about the time he spent at home with his parents. One thing I remember is his description of the young people meeting up at the shop in Trolôn, in the evenings. The shop was kept by John and Ann. Ann had been in service with a family who emigrated to America, and Ann had decided to go with them. Well – John was heartbroken. He decided to follow her. He met up with her in America, they married, and years later, they returned to Wales, and ended up keeping the shop in Trolôn. The young people would listen in amazement to John's stories of America. He told them that once there had been a storm. It was so bad John said, and the wind had been so strong, that it had blown the skin off the cow, and the skin had flown through the air and landed in a tree. With such descriptions, no wonder he had a large audience. Years later, Ann died, once again leaving John on his own. Again, he was heartbroken, and followed her to the place from which no emigrant returns.

My father worked at home on the farm with his parents until he got married.

74

Chapter 7

St James' Church, Rhos, Llangeler

About 1900, some of the people with the same religious per-suasion, and who walked every Sunday to the parish church of St Geler, Llangeler, sometimes failed in their loyalty to their place of worship, and instead turned into one of the chapels lying between them and the distant church. The vicar of the parish became very worried, and decided to call a meeting to see what could be done. All who were interested came together, and they decided to build a small church for the population of Rhos.

The Llysnewydd family gave the field, and on Wednesday, 16th July, 1902, the foundation stone was laid for the new church. A service was held, and the stone laid by Mrs Lewes of Llysnewydd Mansion. Rev. T Jones, Penboyr, Colonel Lewes, Llysnewydd, and Rev. W. Williams, the parish vicar, all spoke. The sermon was given outdoors in the field by Rev. W. Parry Williams, the curate of Cynwyl.

I remember Uncle Dan telling me that he was there. It was a general holiday in the area, and a platform had been erected to act as a pulpit. There were long trestle tables full of food for everyone to have a good time and to celebrate the occasion. Uncle Dan said that everything was going well until the curate of Cynwyl started to preach. At first, he was not too bad. All the children sat on the ground near the pulpit, and behind them were the adults – some sitting, some standing, and some leaning on the hedge. But then the preacher started to work himself up into a 'hwyl' – a frenzy. By this time, he was frothing at the mouth and shouting such things as: 'If you don't behave, you will be punished in hell, and your screams will be heard as far away as Calvary and Gethsemane!' Uncle Dan (who was about eleven years old at the time) said he was so frightened that he couldn't swallow. He worked his way back slowly through the crowd, and hid behind Jams, Brynglas, who was standing by the hedge. At last, the preacher finished his sermon, things returned to normal, and everyone had tea and sandwiches, and enjoyed themselves.

The cost of building the new church was £400. The architect was Mr Thomas Williams, Oaklands, Drefach, and the stonemason was Mr Samuel Jones, Lamb Inn, Llangeler ('Sam Lamb' to his friends), who became a member of St James', and was also choirmaster for many years. The carpenter was Mr E. Thomas, Towyn, Saron.

It was my grandfather, Thomas Jones, Triolbrith, who carried the stones – by horse and cart – from the quarry in

Rhosgeler to build the church. Of course he had help – from Daniel Jones, Blaencwm, Daniel Davies, Rhydiau, John Davies, Blaentriole, and Ben Davies, Ffrydiau Gwynion. The latter became the bell-ringer until his death, in about 1950. Grandfather was churchwarden there for the first 35 years, and also a Sunday School supervisor.

Ben Ffrydiau, as he was known, was a very close friend of my family – he used to come over and help every time Grandfather had a timber sale. Before the day of the sale, a barrel of beer would be brought from the Lamb Inn – in accordance with an established tradition – and kept in the barn. After the sale had finished and most of the people had gone home, if there was any beer left, the helpers would finish off the barrel so that Grandfather could take it back. Sometimes, they would become quite merry, and Ben would start singing. He always began with the same song – 'Y Bwthyn ar y Bryn' (The Cottage on the Hill). These people were hard-working folk who valued the simple things in life.

One item that sticks in my memory is that, on the Sunday following Ben's funeral, the vicar, Rev. Jones-Davies paid tribute to Ben in the following words: 'One of the pillars of St James' Church has fallen.' On the way home, I said to Father, 'I can't see anything wrong with the pillars.' I was then about eight, and, to me, the only pillars I knew were the gate pillars. Father said, 'It shows you were paying attention. You remember what you heard, and one day you will understand what he meant.'

St James' Church, Rhos, Llangeler.

The church was officially opened on Tuesday, 9th June, 1904.

The services were started the previous night in the parish church. The preachers were Rev. Canon Williams of St David's, and Rev. A. Britten, Gorslas. The new church was not large enough to hold the whole crowd of people, so it was decided that the two services should be held outside, in the open air. The sermons, both in the morning and evening, were given by the above preachers, and in the afternoon by the Bishop of St David's.

During the initial meeting when the decision was originally taken to build the church, the vicar was concerned about where people could worship in the meantime, until the church was built. He felt that somewhere should be found in Rhos, to hold services on Sunday evenings. James Davies, Blaennant, Rhos, offered his little cottage for worship until the church was ready. Every Sunday evening at six o'clock, evensong was held in the parlwr at Blaennant. Blaennant was one of the numerous 'tŷ-unnos' cottages that had been built in one night on the common land. As Uncle Dan wrote in '*A Welsh Country Upbringing*' (speaking of the person building the cottage):

> *I wonder if in his wildest dreams he, or any of his helpers, ever thought that they were building more than a human dwelling, as they toiled and stumbled over timber and stone and turf in that unfamiliar light. Did he suspect that on the spot he marked out for the hearth, another was at the same time marking it out for his own 'hearth' and that round this altar he and his friends would kneel to worship the Carpenter of Nazareth? Did angels keep watch this night, and by their presence throw an illuminating glow round the toilers, or at least keep the errant clouds off the face of the moon?*

It became a very prosperous church and full of vigour. With three or four large families it was very easy to fill.

No-one asked to whom the new church should be dedicated. There was no hesitation for one moment. Indeed, from the very first it was called 'St James' after our humble neighbour and host, Jams, Blaennant. This spontaneous and instinctive decision saved the vicar any trouble on the matter. When the time came to dedicate the church, he fell in with the wishes of the people and it was officially dedicated – to the biblical St James, of course. And so the methods of the old rural society had not changed. In the sixth century, a Christian pilgrim and missionary by the name of Celer arrived in these parts and founded our parish church – to be forever called St Celer by the people. In the twentieth century, another helped to found a church which was to bear his name – St James.

There were a few very large families attending the church, namely my own family, the Rhosgeler family, the Blaencwm family, the Etham family, and the Cwmrhyd family. Some of these families had singing in their blood – there were top-rate

My sisters, Mair and Priscilla, going to church, 1947.

tenors, baritones, sopranos, and altos. Therefore, every Calan Hen – which is a festival held every year on 12th January – everybody would come and listen to the singers of St James'. If there were any prizes for singing, St James' singers would win every time.

The church records show that the first wedding took place on 19th February, 1905, between David Morgan and

80

Gwynoro and myself going to Sunday School.

Mother and Father going to church.

81

Mary Davies – both from Pentrecwrt. The first funeral was that of John Davis, Blaentriolau, Rhos, in 1913.

On Thursday, 28th October, 1954, a celebratory service was held in St James' Church to mark the 50th anniversary. The organist was my sister, Priscilla – well, indeed, she was the organist there every Sunday. Incidentally, two of my father's sisters were also organists at St James' – Aunty Sal, and Aunty Liz. All three of my father's sisters were married there, and I include the copies of the original newspaper reports of their weddings:

LLANGELER.

Wedding.—On Saturday last a quiet wedding was solemnised at St. James' Church, Llangeler, by the Rev. Henry Jones, vicar, assisted by the Rev. D. Bonner Jenkins, of St. James. The contracting parties were Miss Sarah Jones, daughter of Mr. and Mrs. Thomas Jones, Triolbrith, Llangeler, and Mr Theo. T. Jones, Blaenbowy, Cilrhedyn, son of Mr. and Mrs. Thomas Jones, Dolwen, Cilrhedyn. The bride, who was neatly attired in a navy blue costume with a grey velour hat to match, was given away by her father. The bridesmaids were Nurse Jones, of a Red Cross Hospital, Birmingham (sister of bride, who wore a navy blue Red Cross uniform, and Miss Lizzie Jones (sister). The duties of best man were carried out by Mr. W. H. Jones (Gwilym Bowy), Gwastod-isaf, Llanpumsaint (brother of bridegroom). After the ceremony the wedding party was entertained to breakfast at the bride's home. The happy couple were the recipients of numerous and costly presents, and carried with them the best wishes of many friends at Llangeler and Cilrhedyn, where they are both very popular.

Report of Aunty Sal's wedding, 1918.

A pretty wedding took place on Saturday, June 23rd, at St. James Church, Llangeler, the bridegroom being Mr. David Evans, Gilwen Farm, Newcastle-Emlyn, and the bride, Miss Lizzie Jones, youngest daughter of Mr. and Mrs. Thomas Jones, Triolbrith, Llangeler. The bride, who was tastefully attired in a navy gabardine costume with a pale blue hat, was attended by her sister (Miss M. Jones, Triolbrith) and Mrs. W. James, Pantymeillion. Mr. Elias Jones, saddler, Newcastle-Emlyn, acted as best man, with Mr. H. Evans (brother of bridegroom) as groomsman. The bride was given away by her father. The Rev. J. Davies (vicar of Llangeler) officiated. The church was tastefully decorated by the lady members of St. James, of which church the bride was assistant organist. The "Wedding March" was played by Miss Davies, Rhydfan. After the ceremony the party left for Swansea via Carmarthen, where the wedding breakfast was partaken of at the Central Hotel.

Report of Aunty Liz's wedding, 1921.

LLANGELER.

WEDDING.—An interesting wedding took place at St. James's Church, Llangeler on the 15th inst., between Miss Mary Jones, eldest daughter of Mr and Mrs Thomas Jones, Ffiolbrith, Llangeler, and Mr. John Davies, Nantygwair Pencader, only son of Mr. and Mrs Samuel Davies, Tyhen, Llangeler. The ceremony was performed by the Rev. D. L. Daniel vicar of Llangeler, assisted by the Rev. O. Davies, curate. Mrs Evans, Rhydygoedfawr Newcastle Emlyn (sister of the bride) presided at the organ and played the "Wedding March." The bride who was given away by her father, was charmingly attired in a crepe-dechine bois de rose dress with velour hat to match, and was attended by three bridesmaids, Miss Sallie Jones, Gellidewyll Farm, Cenarth (cousin of bride) who wore a shrimp coat over a beige georgette dress with velour hat to match, and Misses Margaret and Mary Davies, Tyhen, Llangeler, who were red and navy frocks respectively with black picture hats. The duties of best man were carried out by Mr. D. J. Enoch,

Report of Aunty Mary's wedding, 1927.

Also my own two sisters, Mair and Priscilla, were married there. Now, back to the 50th anniversary service, the guest preacher was my Uncle Dan, and he mentioned how nice it was to be invited back to preach on this very special day, and that he felt very privileged. I remember that the church was so full of people that my brother, Gwynoro, and I had to carry in benches from where they were stored in the shed at the bottom of the churchyard (where the gate is now). Incidentally, another thing that was kept in that shed was the 'elor' – the bier. This was for carrying coffins if they had to be carried for a long way. It consisted of a platform (for the coffin) on four legs, with two shafts to the front and two to the back. I remember asking my father why the long shafts were needed – wouldn't handles be better? He replied that when the coffin was carried for long distances across fields and through narrow places, the bearers would be able to go inside the handles.

Well – back to the big service. The church had been re-decorated for the occasion, and the pine panelling around the walls (which had started to rot due to dampness) was taken out. The bottom of the wall was rendered smooth and painted, and the pulpit was moved from its original position by the altar to its present position. Several gifts were donated to the church to mark the occasion, and I remember some of them. My parents gave one of the chairs at the altar, and the late Anna Mary Williams, Bwlchydomen, gave the other altar chair in memory of her parents – Mr and Mrs D. Jones,

Bwlchclawdd, Llangeler. The carpet at the altar was given by the Rhosgeler family, and the red velvet cover that used to be on the old altar was given by the Triolbrith family. There were also several gifts of money to help with the expense of redecorating, and so on. In fact, every member and also several people with connections with the church gave gifts.

In 1965, new windows were installed in the church. Also, my mother gave the aisle carpet in memory of my father. At about the same time, the pews were replaced because they were beginning to deteriorate. Mrs A. Schofield – originally of Blaencwm – was living in Accrington, Lancashire, and she managed to get pews for St James' from an old chapel which was closing down near where she was living. As a result, the pews at St James' Church are a lot older than the church itself. During the time that Rev. Leslie Woodliffe was vicar of the parish, Mrs Peggy Pugh donated the present altar in memory of her husband, John Pugh, who had been a church-warden at St James. Also, during the time that Rev. Euryl Howells was vicar of the parish, new communion vessels were donated by the present Triolbrith family.

On Sunday, 26th September 2004, there was a big service to celebrate the 100th anniversary of St James' Church. There was an English service in the morning – together with the Harvest Thanksgiving – and at two o'clock, the celebratory Welsh service. During the service, the Bishop consecrated the following: the falls for the reading desk and lectern given by the Derwydd family in memory of their parents, the pulpit fall given by Mrs Gwen Dennis in memory of her family, and the kneelers given by Glyndwr and Nana Lloyd, Tyddyn y Celyn. The church was full, overflowing into a big tent outside in the churchyard. Wayne Mason (Gelliaur, Pencader), who has connections with the church, volunteered to film the service and transmit it on to a large screen in the overflow tent. The organist was, once again, my sister Priscilla, and the guest preacher the Bishop of St David's – the Right Rev. Carl Cooper. After the service, the Bishop, the clergy, the dignitaries and the church members came over here to Triolbrith to have tea. It was quite an occasion, and the day was blessed with fine weather. After tea, there was a cake cutting ceremony by the eldest church member, Mrs Gwen Dennis, together with the Bishop (see photograph, p. 88).

St James' Church still thrives, with a service held there every Sunday. The membership has declined – as in chapels and churches in most parts of the country today. Although we are few in number, we all pulled together to put St James' on the map for the arrangements of the 100th anniversary, despite having no vicar at that time. Just before the service, we were very fortunate to get Rev. Dr. John Gillibrand as our new vicar. This reflected what happened at the 50th anniversary, when Rev. (now Canon) A. J. Davies came to the parish just a few weeks before that anniversary.

At this anniversary, all members worked very hard – the outside of the church was cleaned by pressure washer, new

The Bishop and Gwen, cutting the anniversary cake.

St James' Church today.

guttering was installed, the building was freshly painted inside and out, and various donations were made.

I would like to relate a small item of history at this point – it was before my time, but it was well known by the members of St James'. A 'gentleman of the road' – or some people would call him a tramp – used to sometimes call at the door of the church, and ask whether he could come in to have communion. And the answer was always the same – 'Of course you can'. When he was in the area, he used to stay at Maespant, just down the road from St James', and one winter when he was there, he fell ill, and died. So the members pulled together, and arranged for him to be buried in the churchyard, with a full church burial service. That tells us something about the good people of St James'. Later on, they decided to erect a gravestone, with his name on it, but, alas, they realised that they could only put a curb there, as no-one knew his name or age. The curb is still there, being cared for by the church members to this day. No-one questioned what drove him to become a tramp. All they knew was that he was someone's son, brother, or father. For over a hundred years now the Triolbrith family has worshipped continuously at St James' Church.

The Triolbrith family of my father's generation.

The Triolbrith family of my generation.

91

Chapter 8

THE TRIP TO TONYPANDY

This is a short story that my father told me, and I also heard him telling it to other people, more than once. Mari, Gwarcwm, and Uncle The, Blaenbowi, also told me the same story. It was about a trip they had made to Tonypandy to collect a piano and bring it back to Blaenbowi. Dan Jones, Blaenwaun, was in charge of transport. He was one of the first people in the locality to have a large van. He used to put seats in it, and take people on trips. He also ran a transport service between Bancyffordd and Carmarthen on Saturdays, and, if anyone wanted a van to carry something, he could remove the seats – or some of them – as he did on this occasion.

It was about 1931, just before Christmas, that this journey was arranged. Father started walking from Gwndwn at about three o'clock in the morning – over the moor, and out to meet Dan at the top of Hafod. He was the first passenger. The second was Grandfather, who was ready at the top of the lane. He sat up in the front with the driver. The next to board the vehicle was Mari, Gwarcwm – and I remember her saying how her father, Henry Havard, came with her to the top of Gwarcwm lane to wait for the van. It was pitch dark, but there was no fog. She used to say how she remembered the light of the van turning in at the top of Rhiw Shedi. She also remembered the van stopping at the top of Triolbrith lane to pick up Grandfather. At that time, before the advent of electricity, the countryside at night was pitch black, so that a light coming through the darkness must have been a novelty. Incidentally, Mari had been included in this trip because Grandfather knew that she had an aunt living somewhere in Tonypandy, and he told her that she could come for a day out. The next passenger to get on board was Uncle Tommy, who was, at this time, farming in Llwyn Neuadd, Penboyr. He had walked up to the top of Rhos Llwyn Neuadd to wait for the van. The last passengers were Aunty Sal and Uncle The, Blaenbowi. They had come to a place we used to call 'fingerpost Blaenbowi'. It must have taken careful planning to get them all co-ordinated to meet up, as there were no telephones at that time.

Well, they set off through Hermon towards Cynwyl and on towards Carmarthen. By this time it was around half past five in the morning, with no traffic at all on the road, but going through Carmarthen, they noticed that the town was beginning to wake up. In those days, going from here to Tonypandy and back in one day was quite an achievement. That is the reason they always started off at four o'clock in the morning, and if they returned by midnight, they would only have been away from home for one day.

As they were making their way – I'm not sure where they were, they might have been in Cross Hands, or further – it was still dark. Through the trees they could see a red light, and someone said that a train must be coming. When they drove up to it, the level crossing gate was closed, so Dan put his foot on the brake, but he didn't stop – the brakes failed! So he swerved towards the gatepost and hit it with the long spring that comes out past the front of the van. The gatepost broke, but it stopped the van. As soon as they stopped, an express train hurtled past at top speed. It seems that if Dan had not swerved, they would all have been killed. Dan kept his cool, reversed back a bit, went down under the van and adjusted something. He tried the brakes again, and they were now working, so they went on with their journey.

The crash into the gatepost stayed as a vivid memory for the three people who told me this story. They all felt so lucky to be alive that I never heard how the rest of the day went. I heard the same story from three different people, and they all finished at the same spot. However, I do know that the piano finally arrived safely, because it is still with one of the Blaenbowi family to this day.

Chapter 9

MY MATERNAL GREAT GRANDPARENTS AND THEIR FAMILY

Great Grandfather on my mother's side of the family was called John Jones. He was born in Ffynnonberw in 1839, and died at Bwlchclawdd, Llangrannog, in 1930, aged 91. His mother, my great great grandmother was called Peggy. She used to travel to Llangeitho once a month to have communion. I'm not sure whether she walked, or whether she travelled by pony and trap – whichever way it was, it must have been a big effort, because at that time, the roads were no more than tracks.

John's wife was called Priscilla. She was born at Fronfelen, Penbryn in 1840, and died on 14th October, 1918, aged 78. When they first got married, Priscilla and John lived in a place called Blaendyffryn before moving to Bwlchclawdd, Llangrannog, where they lived for the rest of their lives. They are both buried at Penmorfa Chapel, Llangrannog.

Mother's maternal grandparents – John and Priscilla Jones.

They had six children – three boys and three girls. The first child, Dafydd, was born in 1861, and worked at home on the farm. During the time that he was growing up, several Welsh people were uprooting themselves and travelling to America to seek a better life. Dafydd was only four years old when *The Mimosa* sailed for South America in 1865, with a party of about 150 Welsh people. It is a miracle they survived there, because it was a most uninviting, inhospitable place – they only survived by sheltering in caves for the first winter. Then they eventually settled in Patagonia. In the following years, several hundreds of people moved out there to join them from all parts of Wales, establishing a Welsh colony. These emigrants would write home to their families in Wales, telling them how they were getting on – building new homes, farming, and building better lives for themselves.

Whilst he was growing up, Uncle Dafydd absorbed all this information, and finally decided to move to Patagonia. He didn't have any relatives there at all – I would imagine he was probably hungry for adventure. In 1892, when he was twenty-nine years old, he left. I don't know whether he had any money or not, but he soon got himself some land to farm near Gaiman, and built a house on it which he called Glandŵr. The house still stands there to this day. No doubt he had plenty of help to build his house because masons, carpenters and blacksmiths had also emigrated there. They had all sprung from the same soil – from close-knit Welsh communities, and it was in their blood to support one another – and they flourished and prospered.

Later, Dafydd met a girl called Buddug – her family had gone out to Patagonia from Blaenau Ffestiniog, and they lived on a farm called Gutin Ebrill. Incidentally, it was Buddug's father who won the chair in the first Eisteddfod held in Patagonia. Dafydd and Buddug married in Bethel Chapel, Gaiman, and later they adopted a little girl called Nest. At that time, no-one imagined that Nest would become a relative by marriage – but more about that later, when I write about my Uncle John's life in Patagonia.

There is no doubt that Dafydd did well for himself because, in 1915, he came home to Wales to purchase horses, to improve his stock in Patagonia. He knew that his father had a

Great Uncle Dafydd, Buddug and Nest, outside Bethel Chapel, Gaiman.

good strain of horses, so he arranged the best time to come. It shows how keen a stockman he was – to travel thousands of miles to get new blood of high quality because he was so familiar with that bloodline from when he was growing up. Before he went back to Patagonia, he bought a box full of ladies' hats to take back with him, so that the girls there could wear the same hats as the girls in Wales, to go to chapel.

The second child of my great gandparents was Tomos, born in 1866. He became a builder, and built himself a house called Hawen Villa.

Great Uncle Tomos.

Marged, my grandmother, with the two youngest children,
shortly before she died.

He married a local girl and they had five childen – Mary, Marged, Priscilla Ann, Miriam, and John. Mary often used to come over here to Triolbrith when Mother was here. I always used to enjoy her company.

The third child was Marged, my grandmother. She was born on 25th June, 1871, and died of TB on 28th September, 1914, aged 43. I will write more about her in the following chapter.

The next child was Griffith, born in 1875. He worked at home until he married a local girl called Ann.

100

Griffith.

They moved to a neighbouring farm called Penrallt, lying above the village of Llangrannog. There was a public footpath running through the farmyard of Penrallt, going from the top road into Llangrannog. People used this footpath every Sunday to go to church and chapel. So, every Sunday morning Ann made sure the servant brushed the whole yard clean to give a good impression to people who passed that way. Griffith himself was a very prominent member of the Sunday School in Bancyfelin, Llangrannog, and Mother was so proud of a certificate he had been awarded by the Sunday School in 1905, that she had it framed. He had his award in the Advance Class for the over 21's.

Tom (Morwel) haymaking in Penrallt.

When Griff and Ann retired from Penrallt, they moved to a house called Riverside on the way down to Llangrannog. They had no family.

The fifth child in the family was Ann, born in 1880. She also worked at home until she got married to Evan Lloyd. The couple went to live near Llanelli, where Evan worked in the tinplate industry. I am not sure how long they lived there, but they eventually came home to Bwlchclawdd to run the farm, as Ann's parents were getting on in age. Evan and Ann farmed Bwlchclwdd until their retirement, and finally moved to a house called Tygwyn. They had no family. They often used to come here to Triolbrith. Ann died on 10th September, 1963, and is buried at Penmorfa.

The last person to be born was Sarah Ellen.

Sarah Ellen leading the horse in Bwlchclawdd.

She married Tomos Lewis Davies of Glyngarw. He was a carpenter (see photograph, p. 103), and the couple lived at Morwel which was built on the land at Bwlchclawdd. They had two daughters – Marged Ann, and Mair.

These are all the children of my great grandparents.

Chapter 10

My Maternal Grandparents and their Family

My grandfather, William Jones, was born on 10th September, 1869.

William Jones, Mother's father.

His father, Thomas Jones, was born at Breninlle in the parish of Penbryn, but he had moved to Beili, Llangrannog, by the time that Grandfather was born. Thomas Jones died on 22nd January, 1877. Studying the family bible, one gets the impression that Thomas was someone very religious and upright, and I found this on the flyleaf, written six years before the birth of William, my grandfather:

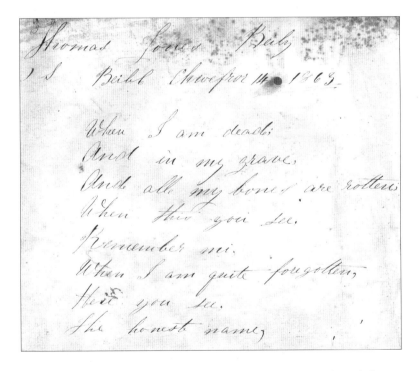

There is no record of his wife anywhere to be found, but I do recall my Aunt, Marged Ann, saying something about her. It seems that, on the death of her husband, she followed the coffin on horseback. This was very unusual, because women used to travel by pony and trap, wearing long black clothes – not 'showing off' on horseback! Neither Mother nor anyone else ever spoke about her.

Thomas Jones is buried at Capel Ffynnon, Plwmp.

It does seem as though Grandfather, William Jones, had a very sad upbringing. His father died when he was only seven years old, and it looks very much as though his mother abandoned him. In any case, he was an only child, and only had one cousin also named William – who farmed at Wstrws at one time. The cousin died in September 1958, and was buried at Pisgah Chapel, Talgarreg.

I have already spoken about Marged, my grandmother (born 25th June, 1871), in the previous chapter. She and William got married on 18th December, 1892, and they eventually settled down and farmed at Beili, Llangrannog.

Their first child was John, born on 21st February, 1893, at Bwlchclawdd, Llangrannog, before the family moved to Beili. John worked at home with his parents until 1914, when he had to join up for the First World War. He served in the South Wales Borderers, first in Europe, and later in the Middle East under Field Marshall Allenby. He was present at the liberation of Jerusalem on Christmas Day, 1917. After the war had ended he returned home. His mother had died on 28th September, 1914, aged 43 years, and his sister, Mary Jane, died on 25th November, 1917, aged 21 years. Both died of TB, and are buried at Capel Ffynnon. I don't know whether or not he was allowed compassionate leave to come home for the funerals. I will write more about John later, when I describe something about his life in Patagonia.

Mary Jane was the second child to be born on 2nd August, 1896.

The third to be born was Thomas – on 26th March, 1898. He married, and the couple had one son called Vincent, who went to live in Abergwili. Vincent is married to Glenys, and they have one son, Alan.

Mary Jane.　　　　　*Thomas.*

Sadly, Thomas died on 2nd March, 1923, aged 25 years, again of TB, and is also buried at Capel Ffynnon.

Uncle Dai (Canada).

The fourth child in the family was David, born 23rd January, 1900.

He worked at home for a while after he left school, then he worked in Ffynnon Werfyl before moving to Blaenshedi. I will

109

write more about David later on, when he went to Canada. Uncle Dai was very keen on attending Sunday School.

Uncle Dai's Sunday School Certificate.

Next came my mother on 14th September, 1901. After she left school she worked at home because her mother had just died, but later went to work in Raybrook Mansion, near Shrewsbury, for Miss Daisy Francesca Wylie.

Miss Wylie also owned Blaendyffryn Hall, Llandysul, Westcliffe Hall, Hampshire, and Ffynnon Wervil, Cardiganshire. Miss Wylie was, at one time, married to Captain William Lewes of Llysnewydd. Mother said that she had

My mother.

enjoyed working in Raybrook for Miss Wylie, although she didn't come home very often because it was quite a distance, and the only way of travelling was by train. I remember her recalling how Miss Wylie used to drive in her Rolls Royce, visiting her estates to keep an eye on things.

111

The next child to be born was Marged Ann, on 29th August, 1904.

Marged Ann.

She was also in service with Miss Wylie for a time, but soon she went to work in London for a family to whom she was recommended by Miss Wylie. Marged Ann never married.

112

She farmed at Calcut, Llanpumsaint, after coming back from London. When she retired, she moved to Bryntweli, Llandysul, where she died on 26th February, 1987. She is buried at Capel Ffynnon.

The sixth child was Griffith, born at Cwmbedw, Rhydlewis, on 3rd June, 1906 – the family had moved there by this time, from Beili.

Griff in Gwndwn.

113

He never married, and spent most of his life with Marged Ann. He died on 10th October, 1995, aged 89, and is also buried at Capel Ffynnon.

Aunty Sally and Uncle Evy on their wedding day.

The last child in the family was Sarah Ogwen (Aunty Sally), born 24th April, 1910, at Blaenbedwfawr, as the family had once again moved to another farm. Sally married Evy son of Dan and Lisa Jones of Blaenwaen, which was a farm on the moor.

The couple moved to farm Nantglas Uchaf, Llanpumsaint, but sadly, Uncle Evy became ill, and was confined to his bed for many years before he died young. They had two children – Megan and Geler. Geler and his family still farm Nantglas today. Aunty Sally died in 1992, aged 82, and is buried with her husband in Llanpumsaint churchyard.

During the time my mother and her brothers and sisters were growing up, they experienced a lot of sadness and disappointments. Despite all this, they attended chapel and Sunday School every Sunday. During the time they lived both in Beili and Cwmbedw, the children attended Rhydlewis School.

On reflection, my mother's father had also experienced a great deal of suffering and loss during his life. I have already mentioned that he lost his parents at a young age. It now seems that he had to endure further loss, with the death of his wife, son and daughter in the space of less than nine years. It must have been a heavy cross to bear. At that time, many young people died in that part of Cardiganshire, from TB. Some of the adults who had contracted the disease isolated themselves from the other members of their family by living in a shed in the orchard or a field near the house. In the case of Mary Jane and Thomas, they had to go into the sanatorium in Tregaron, where they were well looked after. But they finally

Tregaron Sanatorium with Mary Jane (middle row, 2nd from left).

died, and their mother died at home. She knew she was dying and the one thing she would have liked was to take the two youngest children with her. It was a hard time.

When they moved to Blaenbedwfawr, the children went to Gwernlli School, because it was nearer. In 1924, Grandfather and the whole family moved to Blaensiedi Fawr, Bancy-ffordd, which is the next farm but one to Triolbrith, our farm. Because there was no Methodist Chapel in the area, the family decided to attend Capel Mair Church, where they were con-firmed. They became very faithful members, but I don't think they ever forgot their roots in Capel Ffynnon and Rhydlewis. It was at this time that my mother and father met, because

Mother (centre front) and friends at Newcastle Emlyn fair.

Father was working at home here, and Mother was working with her father in Blaensiedi.

I mentioned earlier that I would say a bit more about Uncle John, Mother's eldest brother. Well, after returning home from the First World War, he couldn't settle down, so he decided to leave for Patagonia, where his Uncle Dafydd had settled and had done well for himself.

After arriving in Patagonia, John worked with his Uncle Dafydd on the farm, whose address was 'Glandŵr', Gaiman, Province of Chubut, Argentina, South America. I always looked forward every Christmas to the Christmas card arriving with all the news of the past year. About November time every year, Mother used to post a card to Patagonia, with all our news too. As time went on, John fell in love with Nest – the little girl his Uncle and Aunt, Dafydd and Buddug, had adopted. Eventually, on 24th December, 1924, they married at Bethel Chapel, Gaiman.

By this time, his Uncle Dafydd was ready to retire, so John and Nest took over the farm. They adopted two little girls – Gladys, and Helen de Nora. Later, John and Nest had a son of their own – Ceri. Dafydd and Buddug are buried in Patagonia.

Uncle John was a very respected agriculturalist, and was in charge of the local Agricultural Show, and various other events to do with farming. He was also a well known baritone, singing in the Eisteddfodau and concerts to do with Bethel. Uncle John passed away on 25th January, 1964, aged

John and Nest at their wedding in Patagonia.

The wedding group.

70 years. His funeral service was held at Bethel Chapel, Gaiman.

EMYNAU

I'w canu yn Angladd **Mr. JOHN JONES**
4 fu farw Ionawr 25 1964, yn 70 mlwydd oed.

Ac a gleddir heddiw Ionawr 26, yn mynwent Gaiman

Nes i Dre

Mor agos ambell waith
I dreiddiol olwg ffyd
Yw ty fy Nhad, a phen fy nhaith,
A thoriad nefol ddydd!

    Wyf yma heb ty Naf
    Ymhell o'm nefol wlad,
    Er hyn, bob nos fy mhabell wnaf
    Yn nes i dy fy Nhad.

Yn wastad gyda'm Duw,
    Fy Nhad, boed hyn i mil—
A gad im' yma hefyd fyw
    Yn agos atat Ti:
    Wyf yma heb fy Naf, etc.

Pan rwygo'r llen yn ddwy
    O dan fy olaf chwyth,
Nid angeu fydd fy angeu mwy
    Ond bywyd bery byth.
    "Wyf yma heb fy Naf" etc.

Cael gyda'r Arglwydd mwy
    Byth yn wastadol fod—
O obaith glan! er pob rhwy glwy
    Rwyn disgwyl am ei ddod!
    Wyf yma heb fy Naf, etc.

Craig yr Oesoedd

Rhof fy nhroed y fan a fynwyf
    Ar sigiedig bethau'r byd:
Ysgwyd mae y tir o danaf,
    Darnau'n cwympo i lawr o hyd;
Ond os caf fy nhroed i sengu,
    Yn y storom fawr a'm chwyth,
Ar dragwyddol Craig yr Oesoedd,
    Dyna fan na sygla byth.

Pwyss'r boreau ar fy nheulu,

Colli rhei'ny y prydnawn,
    Pwyso eilwaith ar gyfeillion,
    Hwythau'n colli'n fuan iawn;
Pwyso ar hawddfyd, hwnw'n siglo,
    Profi'n fuan newid byd:
Pwgso ar Iesu,—dyma gryfder
    Sydd yn dal y pwysau i gyd.

Lausanne

Daeth yr awr im' ddianc adre
    Draw o gyrraedd pob rhyw gur;
Gwelaf dorf o'm hen gyfeillion
    Draw ar lân y Ganaan bur.

Dacw'r delyn, dacw'r palmwydd,
    Dacw 'ninnas yn y nef;
Ffarwel bellach bob rhyw ofid,
    Henffych wynfyd yn ei le.

Yno caf fi weled Iesu
    Fyth im' llonni heb un llen,
A chaf yno Ei glodfori
    Byth heb dewi mwy: Amen.

Jesús solo !

Cesarè pisar la tierra,
    Veo la eternidad;
No hay pausa, ni reposo,
    Venga la felicidad,
    En la muerte
No me dejes Salvador.

En el valle de la muerte,
    Con temor alrededor;
¿Quién podrá cambiar mi alma?
    La presencia del Señor;
    Jesús sòlo
En tus manos sonreiré,

Hymn sheet from Uncle John's funeral in Patagonia.

119

His wife, Nest, kept in touch with Mother – giving us all the news from Patagonia. For instance, in 1965, at the celebrations of the 100th anniversary of the Welsh settlement in Patagonia, she sent us a flag celebrating the occasion:

Nest died about 1970, and soon afterwards, their son Ceri also passed away at a young age. Therefore, sadly, we haven't any other relatives in Patagonia, although Gladys, one of the adopted daughters of John and Nest, has been in contact with the family. Nest and Ceri are buried with John in Capel Gaiman.

The other of my mother's brothers to leave for a far distant land was David (Uncle Dai 'Canada'). He sailed from Liverpool on March 18th, 1927, on the *S.S. Doric*.

After he arrived in Canada, he worked for the first two years with some rough characters building railway bridges, so that the old steam trains could cross the rivers – because the railway network was spreading all over Canada at the time. He then met someone who had gone out to Canada from Cardiganshire. This person asked him if he would look after

The S.S. Doric which took Uncle Dai to Canada.

his farm whilst he returned to Wales to visit his homeland. Soon after that, Uncle Dai bought what was called 'a quarter section of land' from the government – this consisted of 160 acres, and he bought it at $3.00 an acre. He built a cabin on it, and called it Dixonville. He started farming – cattle and horses. He couldn't keep sheep because of the coyotes and wolves. In 1964, Uncle Dai came home for a couple of months for the first time since 1927, and it was very interesting to hear his tales of Canada. The winters were very hard and long. It would snow for days at a time, and he would be cut off for three months in the winter. He enjoyed life in Canada. Every six weeks or so, when there was no snow, he and a few

of his neighbours would drive by jeep to Calgary or Edmon-
ton for the week-end to visit the rodeos and horse races,
because horses were the love of his life. I remember him
describing how the native Indians would always help with the
harvest and various other jobs in summer. In the winter, they
would disappear deep into the forests, and would not be seen
for weeks at a time.

Uncle Dai 'Canada'.

When I was growing up, I always looked forward to his
Christmas cards with all his news. I can still remember most
of them – I remember the one saying 'Remember me to
Johnnie, Triolmawr, and Dafydd, Blaennantrhys'. He always
ended his cards or letters to Mother with 'from your loving
brother, Dai.' His address was 'Dixonville', Clear Hill, Peace
River, Edmunton, Alberta. Uncle Dai passed away on 17th
February, 1966. I remember the telegram arriving:

Uncle Dai was cremated in Canada, and his ashes returned home for burial with the rest of his family at Capel Ffynnon. Having two brothers so far away, I am sure Mother must have missed them, and longed to see them. On the other hand, they kept in touch regularly, and it widened all our horizons, getting news at first hand from distant places.

Chapter 11

Father and Mother

Father and mother married on the 12th June, 1927, at Capel
Mair Church, with Uncle Tommy as best man.

Father and Mother on their wedding day.

Aunty Sally and Griff with Father and Mother in Gwndwn.

They then moved to Gwndwn Gwyn above Cwmduad in
the parish of Cynwyl Elfed, in order to start farming on their
own. Gwndwn is an upland farm of about 100 acres, with the
top fields going up as far as Cruglas – an ancient burial mound
lying on the boundaries of the parishes of Llangeler and Cynwyl. From Cruglas, water runs down in a northerly direction
to the Cardigan Bay, and in a southerly direction to the Carmarthen Bay. Rhos, Llangeler, used to lie on open moorland

125

up as far as Cruglas, Garn Wen, and Crug Bach until 1967, but at that time almost all of the area was planted with trees by the Forestry Commission, and spoiled.

My parents lived in Gwndwn for nine years, and their three eldest children were born there. Mair was born on 8th September, 1931, and was christened Margaret Mary – the names of her two grandmothers. Priscilla was born on 19th July, 1933. Her full name, Priscilla Ann, comes from my mother's maternal side of the family. The first Priscilla known to us was my mother's grandmother. It was also my mother's name. Gwynoro, my brother, was born on 28th March, 1936. His full name is William Thomas Gwynoro – his first two names are the names of his two grandfathers, and Gwynoro

Gwndwn, as it is today.

126

was one of the five saints of Llanpumsaint. The three of them were christened in St Albans Church, Cwmduad – where my parents were faithful members during their time at Gwndwn.

I am the only person to be born here at Triolbrith on the 29th June, 1940. I was christened Peter Winston at St James' Church – Winston because Winston Churchill had become Prime Minister, very much the same as when my mother's father was born in 1869, he was given the name William when William Gladstone was Prime Minister. I was given the name Peter because St Peter's Church, Swansea (where Father used to worship when he worked there) had just been bombed. Sadly, my parents lost three infants before I was born, and they are buried at St James'.

My sister Mair can remember some of the things in Gwndwn (she was only five when the family left there). She can remember the pond, the water wheel, the garden, and the long lane leading to the farm from Cwmduad.

I can remember my parents talking about many people who were neighbours of theirs in Gwndwn – Tom and Ann (Penrhiwlas), Esther (Llechseion), and Jane (Nantyfen). One winter, after Tom and Ann had moved away from Penrhiwlas down to Cwmduad, the roof of Penrhiwlas was blown off during a storm. So the people who lived there at the time – Mr and Mrs Edwards and their children – moved into Gwndwn to live with my parents for three or four months until the roof had been repaired. The Edwards family later moved to Penralltwen, nearer Cwmduad.

In 1936, as I said, my parents moved back to Triolbrith because my grandparents were retiring from farming and moving to live in Abernant – a house about 100 yards down the main road from St James' Church.

My grandparents, just before they retired.

The auctioneer for the farm sale was Lloyd and Thomas of 1 Blue Street, Carmarthen. Something worth mentioning here is that Mr Jones, the Headmaster of Brynsaron School, decided to come to the sale. Because the sale was held on a weekday, Mr Jones left the girls with the infant teacher, Miss Evans, to do needlework, and brought all the boys from his class with him to the sale. Two of the boys who came with him were Cyril (Derwydd) and Les (Maengwyn). Later, they both told me about coming to the sale that day, because it had been so memorable to them.

Father and Mother soon settled down here because Father had been accustomed to come over to Triolbrith from Gwndwn to help his father with various jobs. After Grandfather retired to Abernant, he in his turn would come over to Triolbrith to help Father with the harvest and other work. Abernant happened to be on the way to school, and my sister, Mair, found it convenient to take the pony and trap to Abernant, and walk the rest of the way to school. Then Grandfather would use the pony and trap to come back here, to save walking – because, by this time he was getting on, and not feeling as young as he had been. When Mair came home from school, she used to stay with Grandmother at Abernant until Grandfather returned with the pony and trap in the evening – which she would then use to travel the rest of the way home. Those were the days before motor cars.

My parents started selling milk about 1940 (before that, all the milk had been used to produce butter and cheese, and sold that way). The milk churns had to be carried out by pony and trap to the Bancyffordd road, where the milkstand stood – we shared the milkstand with Triolmawr.

Haymaking.

The Standard Fordson.

In 1942, Father bought a new Standard Fordson tractor, which is still here, and a three-furrow plough.

He would then plough as much in a day as he had done with the horses in a week. Later on he bought a lorry to cart hay and corn, but I don't think that was very successful. The lorry was later dismantled, and the axle and wheels used to make a trailer for the tractor. About 1944, my parents bought their first car from Uncle Har who was the car's first owner, but because of the war and the petrol shortage, Uncle Har was forced to sell it. So, Father bought it – a green Morris 10, registration No. TH 3726. It was one of the first cars in the area.

The old Morris with Uncle Davey and Aunty Agnes.

Later on, Father bought another tractor – an International Farmall – and that brought an end to the horses working on the farm. In 1954, our first milking machine was installed. In 1956 my brother, Gwynoro, got married and moved away from home. My two sisters were already married by this time, so I returned from Rhyddgoedfawr – where I was working at the time – to work on the farm with my parents. I have been here ever since. Priscilla married Elwyn Jones, of Gaerwen Uchaf, Mair married Alcwyn Jones, of Penlan, and Gwynoro married Rita Jones of Treale.

During the time I was working with my parents, the stable was turned into a cowshed, and we did away with the pigsties. At that time, a revolution was taking place in farming, heralding the end of a way of life that hadn't changed appreciably since the time of the Romans. I remember my father telling me that, when he was a boy, he remembered his mother telling him to go and count how many people were in the field cutting hay with scythes, so that she could prepare the food for the workers. He said that he had counted seventeen cutting in the field at the same time.

When I was growing up, and later when I was working at home, there was one very exciting time of the year – potato picking. All the local farms would co-operate over potato week – one farm would book one day, another would book the next, and so on, for the whole week. Our time was spent going from one farm to another, all neighbours coming

A common scene at the time.

Potato picking at Bwlchyddwyrhos – about 1942.

together to combine their efforts. Our circle was as follows: Glyncoch, Blaenpant, Bwlchyddwyrhos, Blaensiedi, Triolmawr, Triolbrith, Gaerwenuchaf, Tymaen, Bwlchclawddmorgan, and Rhosgeler.

Another exciting time was threshing day. This took place twice a year – in Spring and Autumn. Again, as with potato week, it would not have been possible without the goodwill, team effort, and co-operation of the neighbouring farmers.

Feathering was also a very special day, because my parents used to breed geese, turkey, and chickens for the Christmas market. They had the same customers from one year to the next – their customers were obviously very satisfied with the produce because they came from as far afield as Cardiff and the Rhondda. Plucking and feathering took place in our 'gegin fach', and after dressing the birds, Mother would store them in the 'llaethdy' (the dairy) as it was cool on the slate slabs. The following day, I had to go and deliver geese wings to Ann (Ffynnonfach), Ruth (Brynglas), and Ann (Erwlon) – they used them for dusting. The two ladies that had been regular 'pluckers' from before my time were Marie (Gwarcwm) and Annie (Cware). They were two cheerful, big women, who used to talk and laugh from early morning until late in the evening. It was a very long day for them because feathering had to be done in one day. This was because the next day customers would be arriving to collect the poultry, and also Father would have to take some of the poultry to the railway station to be dispatched to other customers.

134

Planting potatoes.
Back row, left to right: Marged (Triolmawr), Annie (Cware),
Marie (Gwarcwm), Gwynoro.
Front row, left to right: Mair, Winston, Priscilla.

In the summer, my parents would take the women helpers out for the day in the car. It was usually a day out in Swansea and Mumbles, as a reward for their loyalty. Indeed, they came often to help with other things, such as planting the potatoes, and sorting them.

Annie was also present here the day I was born, and she always used to tell me that she washed me for the first time. I was very privileged to be one of the bearers at her funeral at Penboyr Church. She had been a pillar of strength to my parents for many years. She could always find a word of wisdom to make someone feel better, no matter what the circumstances. The world is a lot poorer without her.

Gwynoro, myself and Father, about 1946.

In 1958, my father's health began to fail. He had had a bad chest after being gassed in the Great War in Germany, and his mother always used to say that he coughed every day after returning home. In August 1960, he and I were cutting corn in Parcgwyn when he became very ill. Mother nursed him through the winter with the help of my two sisters, and on 1st March, 1961, at 10.30 a.m. he passed away. Mother, Gwynoro, and I were with him. His funeral took place at St James' Church the following Saturday, where a very large crowd of people had gathered to pay their last respects.

136

He was sadly missed by all who knew him over a wide area. One thing which stays in my memory is that it was very warm for the time of year, and all the daffodils had opened early in our lane, as if to say 'goodbye and thanks' – for it was he who had planted them.

I remember Rev. A. J. Davies paying tribute to him at his funeral. He remembered him as a true friend and a loyal neighbour, with such wide interests that he could converse on many topics. My father was a man of many skills. For instance, I remember how he used to build big corn stacks and thatch them with such skill and precision. When he ploughed, every furrow was turned, and every row opened with such accuracy, as though taking part in a competition. I remember his passing with much sadness. I was twenty years old at the time.

Chapter 12

UP TO THE PRESENT DAY

After Father died, Mother and I stayed on here to farm. I got married in 1964 to Janet Richards of Penrallt Ddu, Hermon, and Mother retired to Towyn Cottage, Saron. We had two children – Helen (born 16th March, 1965) and Colin (born 8th January, 1969). Little did I know at the time that within six years of getting married I was going to suffer the greatest loss in my life so far, by the passing of my dear wife and mother of my children on 21st June, 1970, when she was only 28 years old. She is buried at Hermon Chapel, Cynwyl Elfed.

My mother came back to live with me for four years, to help me bring up the children, and for that I am forever indebted to her, for her kindness and love. She must, at that time, have thought that history was repeating itself, for her father had suffered losses in similar circumstances when she was a young girl growing up in Rhydlewis. Because of that experience, she was able to be so strong and give so much of herself, to support me. Mother spent the last three years of her life in Erwhir Residential Home in Carmarthen, where

Helen.

she was well looked after. She passed away on 13th March, 1992, aged 91. Mair and Priscilla were with her. She is buried at St James, with my father.

Helen was married and lived in Pembrokeshire. She has one daughter, Stephanie. Her marriage to Andrew Reynolds ended, and she now has found happiness with her new partner, James Morgan. They are currently building a new house in Spittal, Pembrokeshire.

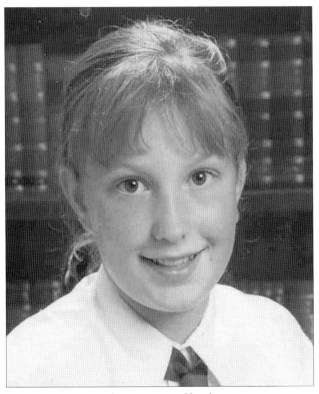

Stephanie, my granddaughter.

Colin.

Colin joined the army into the Royal Engineers when he left school in 1985, at the age of 16. He saw active service in Iraq during the liberation of Kuwait in 1991. Soon after that he was in the Bosnian war, and later in Kosovo. He has also been stationed in Gibraltar, Canada, Germany, Cyprus, and Kenya, before spending seven months serving in Basra,

Southern Iraq in 2004. In 1999 he married Julie Martin of West Sussex, and she has been stationed with him in Cyprus for two years. He has now reached the rank of Warrant Officer, Class 2. I remember a couple of months before their marriage, Colin and Julie came here, to Triolbrith, for the weekend. Colin asked me to be his Best Man. Well, I was a bit surprised, as I knew he had plenty of close friends in the Army. He explained: "Because you have always been there for me." So it was a great privilege to be there for him once again when they married at All Saints' Church, Crawley Down, West Sussex, on 7th August, 1999.

On 6th September, 1992, I was again delivered a sad, tragic blow by the sudden and unexpected death of my youngest

Mark, aged 17.

son, Mark, at the age of seventeen – the son I had from my second marriage, which ended with that tragedy.

I think it was the faith and strength that I inherited from my parents and grandparents that pulled me through, and also the support that I had from Helen and Colin and my brother and sisters.

Since then, the wheel of time has turned, I have moved on, and on 5th April, 1999, at Capel Mair Church, I married Gillian, the daughter of Rev. and Mrs R. E. Hughes, of North Wales. Without her help with the typing, this script would have not seen the light of day.

Chapter 13

CONCLUSION

To end this chronicle, I would first like to remark on the obvious importance of religion to our ancestors. When I visit the places where my antecedents are buried, I can almost sense the presence of the intangible quality which made them the way they were – very hard working, and very loyal to each other. Another characteristic was their unswerving loyalty to the Crown – they were all staunch Royalists. I suppose this fitted in well with their strict way of life.

We must remember that before the advent of the Welfare State people had to be much more self-sufficient. Everyone, for instance, had to pay for the doctor's services. Unfortunately when people were poor, sometimes the doctor wouldn't be called until it was too late. As a consequence, people were very keen to make their own home-made remedies for different ailments and aches and pains. They also made their own jams, preserves and wine, and I enclose some examples of these recipes from my own family at the end of this chapter. I also enclose some of the advertisements that were in the newspapers at the beginning of the nineteen hundreds, advertising some of the gadgets for the home.

It is worth passing on every little detail of one's family and ancestry because one day, in many years to come, it will become a part of history. A perfect example of this comes from the Maddan tribe of North American Indians in Canada. There, the older people of the tribe have handed down the story of how, in the eleventh century, Madoc, son of Owain Gwynedd, sailed with the Vikings from North Wales to North America (now Canada). Incidentally, Madoc sailed with the Vikings because his mother was a Viking girl from Scandinavia. Owain Gwynedd and his son Madoc sailed from Porthmadog (hence the name) and discovered America – contrary to the common belief that Columbus discovered it much later. The elders of the Maddan tribe handed down stories of how the long narrow boats arrived, and they always mentioned the wolf's head carved on the prow. Apparently, these boat trips happened many times over a period of about twenty years for trading purposes, the route being North towards Greenland and the Arctic Circle, then across in a westerly direction, and finally South to the East coast of – what is now – Canada. Very often some of the Welsh would stay on with the Indians, and some of the Indians would sail with the crew back to Wales, to stay for a while, and visit Anglesey. That is the reason why, somewhere on the East coast of Canada, there is a tribe still using several Welsh words in their vocabulary. Also, because of the influence of the Viking blood, Indians can be seen having blue eyes and blonde hair – features unknown in any other Indian tribe. The reasons for these phenomena would have been lost had not the tribal elders passed down the information to future generations, when they sat round their camp fires. No matter how insignificant the material seems that we pass on, one day someone will value it and preserve it.

REMEDIES

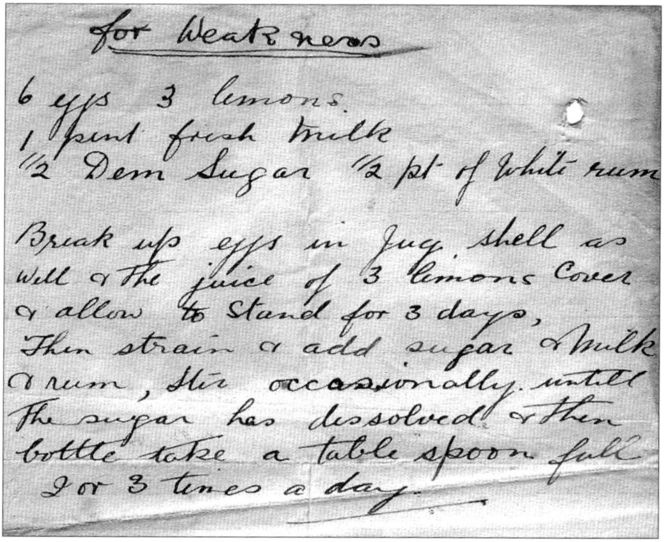

for Weakness

6 eggs   3 lemons.
1 pint fresh milk
1/2 Dem Sugar 1/2 pt of White rum

Break up eggs in jug, shell as
well & the juice of 3 lemons Cover
& allow to stand for 3 days,
Then strain & add sugar & milk
& rum, Stir occasionally. until
the sugar has dissolved & then
bottle take a table spoon full
2 or 3 times a day.

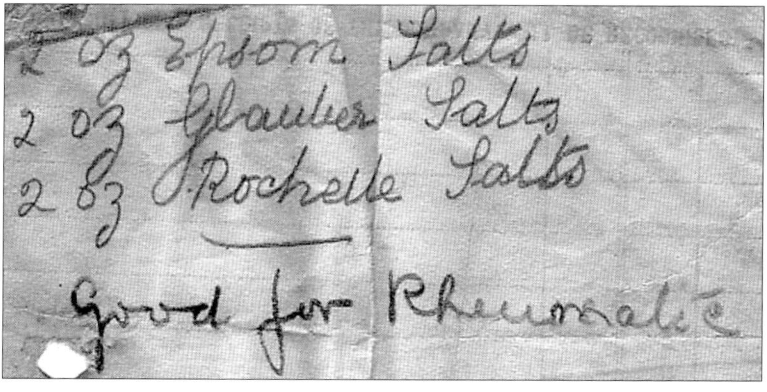

2 oz Epsom Salts
2 oz Glauber Salts
2 oz Rochelle Salts

Good for Rheumatic

147

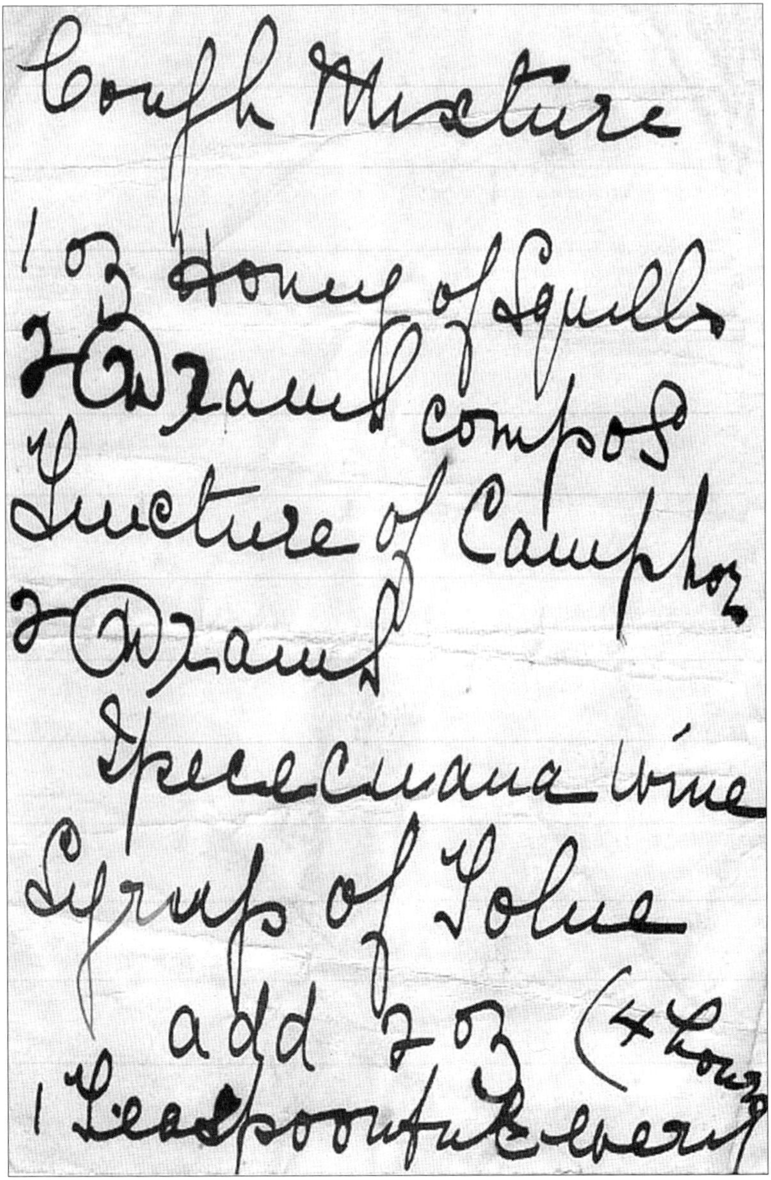

Cough Mixture

1 oz Honey of Squills

2 Drams compos

Tincture of Camphor

2 Drams

Ipececuana wine

Syrup of Tolue

add 7 oz (4 hour

1 Teaspoonful every

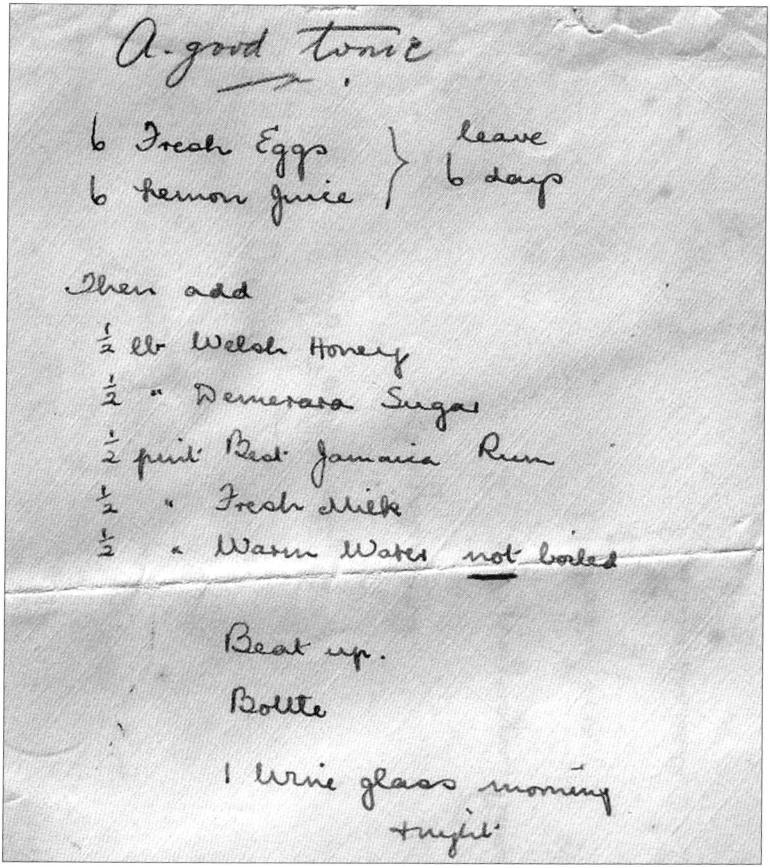

A good tonic

6 Fresh Eggs   leave
6 Lemon Juice   6 days

Then add

½ lb Welsh Honey
½ " Demerara Sugar
½ pint Best Jamaica Rum
½ " Fresh Milk
½ " Warm Water not boiled

Beat up.

Bottle

1 wine glass morning
          + night

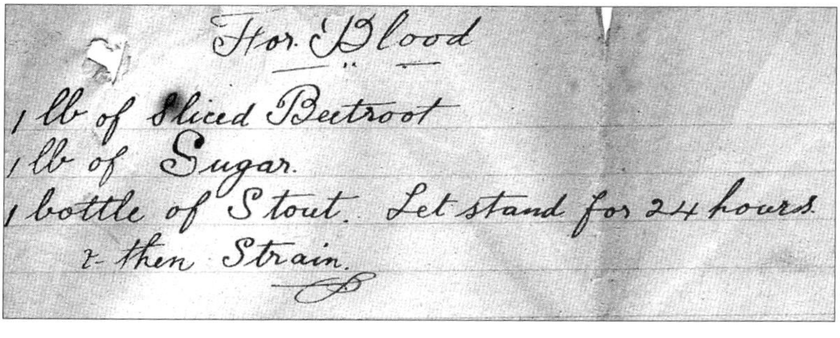

For Blood

1 lb of Sliced Beetroot
1 lb of Sugar.
1 bottle of Stout. Let stand for 24 hours.
   & then Strain.

149

Recipes for Wine Making

Elder Berries Wine

⅟₄ lbs of clean berries to every qrt of
water, soak the berries in the water
for 9 days & stir them once every day
then strain the berries from the water
no boiling on the berries, measure
your quanity of wine, boil qrt or more
of it to put with cloves spices ginger
lemon few raisens, boil for half an hour
put 3 lbs of sugar to every gallon of wine
pour this on the sugar when it comes to
warm to and a slice of Bread put on the
top of Bread a little yeast to work for 9 day
put little of isinglass.

The recipe for the
Whiskey is as follow:
1 lb Demerera Sugar
1 lb Raisens
1 lb Pearl Barley
Let it stand for 14 days in a gallon of cold
water then strain, bottle, and allow it to
work. Mr Williams B. Bond was saying today
that he strained & bottled his yesterday. but
there not much color on it and he is going to ask
the person if there is something wanted to color it
so we shall let you know again what he will
say. Best love to you both from us all

150

Parsley Wine

¾ lbs of Parsley
4 " " Lump Sugar.
1 Gallon Water
2 oz lump Ginger
½ oz Yeast
2 Lemons.

Choose good green parsley
plucked from the stalks.
Boil parsley for half an hour, then
strain, add sugar, and ginger well
(bruised) & lemons sliced, and
boil for another hour. Stand
in a bowl until lukewarm,
& spread yeast on toast. Leave
in a warm place for 24 hrs.
then put in a gallon jar for
six weeks. strain bottle again
& cork well down.

Elder Flower Wine   Mrs J. (Recipe)

1 gallon water , 1½ lbs raisins
4 lbs sugar ½ oz yeast.

Gather the flowers on a dry day + hang up to dry for
2 or 3 days. Take the flowers off the stalk and
measure - putting 1 qt of water to a pint of
flowers. Place the raisins , flowers + water on
to boil for about an hour.
            Take off + strain. Measure the
liquid and put 3¼ lb sugar to each pint
of liquid + boil for another hour.
            Take off + pour into a pan, putting
about 1/2 oz yeast spread on bread on the
top. Allow it to remain in the pan for a
few days. Then bottle. but do not cork
for another 9 days. It can be kept
for any length of time.

Recipe No 2.   Elderty bloom wine

1 qt of flowers to one gallon of water
3 lbs   sugar.   "   "   "
2 lemons   ½ oz of yeast.
1 lb raisins .
Boil flowers , raisins + lemons for 2 hours.
Strain off + return to boil with sugar for
½ hr. Work in the usual way.

152

Dandelion Wine

4 qts Dandelion Flowers
4 " Boiling Water
3 lbs Loaf Sugar
1 inch of whole ginger
1 Lemon, 1 thinly peeled rind of orange
1 oz yeast moistened with water

Method

Put petals of flower into a bowl, pour over them the boiling water and allow to stand 3 days. Stir frequently. Strain liquid into pan, add rind of orange & lemon, sugar & ginger. Boil gently for ½ hour & when cooled add yeast spread on piece of toast. Allow to stand 2 days   Bottle for use.

Blackberry Wine.

To every Pint of Blackberries add 1 pint of boiling water. Pour the boiling water over the fruit which has been put in an earthenware pan. Stir every day. for a fortnight Then strain, and to every gallon of juice add 3½ lbs of lump sugar Stir until sugar dissolves, allow to stand 3 days longer. when wine will work, then bottle but do not cork tightly for 3 months.

153

Elderflower Champagne.

Ingredients.

2 heads of elderflower, in
full bloom. 1 gallon cold water,
1 Lemon. 1½ lb. sugar. 2 tablespoon
-fuls, of white Vinegar.

Squeeze the juice of Lemon cut
the rind in four. Put this
with the Elderflower and
Vinegar in a large ~~bottle~~.
basin. pour on the cold
water. steep. for 24 hrs.
Strain off and bottle in
Screwed top bottles. and
keep for 2 wks at-
least before using.

Parsnips Wine

3 lbs of Demera sugar
4 " Parsnips
¼ z Hops
1 Table spoon of yeast
1 Slice of Tosted Bread
4 quarts of Boiling water.

Boil the parsnips gentle in the water for
fifteen minutes add the Hops & cork for
ten minutes longer strain add the sugar
Let in liquid become Lugal & pout n
the toast spread with yeast, let it sta-
for 36 Houses then, turn into a cask. which
should fill strain as soon as possible as
permutation closes strain into small Bottle
cork & store for one month before useing

154

Some Newspaper and Shop Advertisements in the Early 1900's

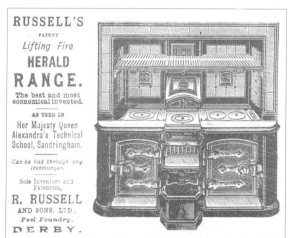

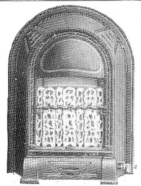 

SUPREME IN QUALITY.

ODOURLESS

"Chiswick Imperial"

SOFT SOAP

The Best thirty years ago and
Unapproachably The Best to-day.

MAKES EASY WORK OF SCRUBBING AND SCOURING.

OF ALL GROCERS EVERYWHERE.

OAKEY'S SPECIALITIES.

WELLINGTON KNIFE POLISH.
Prepared for Oakey's Patent Rubber Knife Boards and all Patent Knife-Cleaning Machines. In Canisters, 3d., 6d., 1s., 2s. 6d., and 4s. each.

" POLYBRILLIANT " ROUGE POMADE.
For Cleaning all Metals. In Tins, 1d., 2d., 3d., and 6d. each.

WELLINGTON BLACK LEAD.
The Best for Polishing Stoves, Grates, and Ironwork, without waste, dirt, or dust. In 1d., 2d., and 4d. Blocks; and 1s. Boxes.

FURNITURE CREAM.
For Cleaning and Polishing Furniture, Patent Leather, Oilcloth, etc. Glass and Stone Bottles, 6d. and 1s.

BRUNSWICK BLACK.
For Beautifying and Preserving Stoves and all kinds of Ironwork. Bottles, 6d., 1s., an6 2s.

SILVERSMITHS' SOAP.
(Non-Mercurial) for Cleaning and Polishing Silver, Electro-Plate, Plate Glass, Marble, etc. Tablets, 6d.

Sold Everywhere by Ironmongers, Grocers, Druggists, Oilmen, &c.

JOHN OAKEY & SONS, Ltd., LONDON, S.E.

Coal Merchants

— TO —

His Majesty

The King.

Write

for

Prices.

Enquiries Invited for truck loads to Country Stations.

RICKETT, COCKERELL & Co., Ltd., TOWER HOUSE, TRINITY SQ., LONDON, E.C.

161

LETTERS RECEIVED FROM UNCLE DAN

I mentioned earlier that I intended editing and publishing some of Uncle Dan's letters to me, and here are a few of the many that I received from him. I am publishing these letters as a token of gratitude, and as a tribute to him. His love of Triolbrith, St James' Church and Capel Mair is evident from these letters.

18 Allt-yr-Yn Crescent,
Newport,
Gwent.
NP7 5GD

April 10th, 1976

My dear Winston,
Here are two more photographs that really ought to find their place at Triolbrith. In the group I can see Uncle David

and Uncle Henry sitting down. Who is the other on the left?

From left to right – Great Uncle Sami, Father, Heulwen, Aunty Agnes, Mother, Uncle Dai, Uncle Har.

I trust you are all keeping well. As for myself, I have nothing to complain of. In the summer, all being well, Kate and I are coming to see you, and to see the place where I was brought up. She, of course, is a farmer's daughter. I find great pleasure now in looking at photographs we took early, when the children were small, and of course they are being distributed to them now. Keep a record of the family as they grow up. I wish we had a little more sunshine. I do not think the farmers would consider it a good spring. All good wishes,

Uncle Dan

June 7th, 1976.

My dear Winston,
Here is some reading material for you. When I say talk to others about these things, I mean the things concerning the old roads, and the stories about a church being there, and the apparitions. The things about the farm are only of interest to the family. I have no news – Kate and I are well. I hope you can say the same about your family.

Written for Winston Jones, Triolbrith, Llangeler.

I shall write this partly in Welsh as the mood takes me. You are the only one, it seems to me, who takes an interest in things concerning the farm, the people and the locality generally. I had a very good memory and liked to listen as father and mother and the neighbours generally spoke about old times old things, and old happenings.

I hope you will preserve what I am going to tell you, and I think you will. Talk to the children about them – and to others too; the more people who know about them, the more the knowledge will spread. And keep these notes safely, and after your day they will go down to your children.

First of all about the farm: you will know what a difficult pitch Rhiw fach is. In the old times it would seem that the farmers at Triolbrith did not take the carts up it, but turned into Cae Gwair Ucha, and then across that field to the farm. In the top hedge of the field near the bottom of the pitch the Bwlch (gap) is still to be seen. It has been filled up of course, and was never used in father's time. Cae Gwair Ucha was hardly ever ploughed. It was so handy to turn the animals to, and it was near the farm. But I remember father ploughing it and putting the usual crops in it in their usual order. I helped in all this as a boy I should think of about fourteen. When he was ploughing it, he discovered that there was a harder stretch – you could hardly call it a road, going from that gap in the hedge across to the farmyard.

Cae Gwair Ucha was once two fields, a hedge ran down from the hedge of Parc yr Ardd right down to the bottom; some evidence of that hedge may be seen in the above hedge to this day. When the field was two, the name of the top field was Parc dan Rhiw. You will know the names of the four fields you have made into one: they were Parc Garreg Wen, Parc Eben, and above them Parc y Berth and Parc Cenol Ucha. Until I was about twenty there was a huge white stone (carreg wen) in the middle of the field. It was blown up at that time by a brother-in-law of Mr Evans (Evans bach as we called him, he lived at Brynteg and was our Lay Reader for many years at St James). He came often to Triolbrith. He was later ordained, became in the end the vicar of Llanhowell in Pembrokeshire. He became blind and retired to Carmarthen. They had one girl who gave them much sorrow in their old days, and much trouble to the police.

Parc Eben got its name from the fact that it was once used by Eben Havard, the father of Henry Havard, Gwarcwm. When the <u>Small Holdings Act</u> was passed, your grandfather was greatly troubled, in case they might remember that, and seek to have it again. But he heard nothing.

You might wonder how Parc Cenol Ucha had that name because it is not in the middle, but in my grandfather's time, another field now belonging to Cwmnant Einon belonged then to Triolbrith. At the top end of the further hedge, you will still see at the top the entrance to it from Parc Cenol Ucha. You have brought the Waun under cultivation – good for you. During the First World War, the government sent a man with a tractor to try and plough it, but because of the stones, the tractor was almost always in need of repair, and the job was given up.

When the Common of Rhos Llangeler was divided, the two top fields (Y Waun and Parc Main were part of the Common and were given to the church of Llanddarog (that is to the Vicar) as he was a landowner in the parish. They were fenced in in time, but not much use was made of them until father's time. It was he who planted with beech the top hedge of Rhoswar Fach. Blaentriole was given to Col. Lewis, and Triolmaengwyn to Jones Penrallt, and they built the farm buildings on them and fenced the land in. The Common reached down to Clais then, and the road that came up from Pentrecwrt turned right where Clais now is.

I think father told me that he remembered the Common an open country, and lowland farms, like Cwrt, used to send their cattle up there. They were probably the younger cattle, but they had not much life up there, and possibly ended up as runts.

The top enclosed and cultivated farms were Triolmawr, Triolbrith, Cwmnant, Gaerwen Uchaf, Bwlch, Tyhen, Waun-lwyd, Bwlch Clawdd, and Blaengilfach. The rest had been common land until it was begun to be built upon.

The land on the North of the road that goes from near Belon across to St James, that is to a depth of a field or so, was common land. The field on which St James' Church was built was given to the Vicar of Llangeler. Cwmins bach was given to the parish for the purposes of recreation. The top fields of Triolbrith farm at this time (before the enclosure of the common) were Rhoswar Fach and Rhoswar Fawr.

When I was a boy there was a gate between Triolbrith and Cwmnant at the far end of Parc Eben. There was also a gate between Triolmawr and Blaenshedi, and there was another further on, referred to as Iet Rhydshedi. There also had been one on top of the lane coming off from Triolbrith, as you turned left towards Rhiwfach. Evidence will be seen on the Parc-yr-Ardd side. Father did away with the opposite portion of hedge when he straightened the road there.

It seems that at one time Triolbrith Farm was rebuilt a little bit higher up. The ruins of the old buildings can still be seen below the farm, and that part was always called 'Clos Isha'. Father built that short hedge before the gate (in Cae Gwair Ucha) and planted trees on it. Below it, on the East side of that sycamore tree was the old Odyn, or Odyn mâs, in which they dried the grain. One belonged to every farm in those days, and there is generally a 'Cae'r Odyn' near every farm.

The 'pwll llifio' was at the top of the orchard opposite the small window at the North end of the old gegin fach, now the lavatory. I remember our neighbours walking around 'Clos Isha' at haymaking time, examining the ground, because they believed that there had once been a church there, and the unevenness of the ground looked very much like grown-over graves. At one time, a conifer tree – larch or pine, or some similar tree – grew there, but it was not a yew tree, as the people believed. I remember it well, a straight tall tree, but it had then begun to wither, and in the end, father cut it down for firewood.

The tradition of a church there was very persistent. It was said that a young girl, coming up from Cwmcerrig late at night for a bottle of milk, saw – when she came to the top of

Parcgwastod – a priest in his white robes going across in front of her, reading the Litany. She got so frightened that she ran all the way back – and not much good became of her after that. Could there have been some sort of church there? I have never seen such a lot of stones (stone hedges) as around Triolbrith Farm. Where did they all come from? Were they part of some original building, now forgotten?

When we were young we used to cut across Parc Gwyn to the top corner and over a Canfa, there, down into the Allt, along a well trodden path down to the river, cross it at a pool which we called <u>Pwll y Badell</u>. It is quite a big pool, and I remember bathing in it on a hot summer day. After crossing the river here, we would travel up through the lane there and out to Belon (now Gaerwenog). It saved a lot of time, if we wanted to go to shop Trolon, or to Jim Saer.

Many crossed in those days from Bwlchyddwyrhos, through clôs Blaenshedi, Triolmawr and Triolbrith, and out to Belon. It saved them some walking, but there was never a recognised path or way along there. But father was once bothered because a lot of different people lived at different times at Blaentriolau, and they used to cut down through Parcmain and the top right corner of Rhoswar Fawr and over the hedge to Cwmnant field. Other people coming up from Cefen Gilfach and Llanpumsaint area might find out about it, and begin to use it. I don't think father made them sign a paper (except perhaps in the case of one, or threatened to do so) to the effect that they were allowed to cross with his permission. They had no right to go that way. In time, Blaentriolau was abandoned, and nobody came that way again.

In order to manure the steep sides (bronnau) of fields like Parc Ribyn father had a carllusg made by Jim Saer, with iron on the sides on which it ran. There were no shafts; the horse was just hitched to it. It could therefore run, and one had to be very careful.

When change of vicars came to Llanddarog, the diocesan architect, or some such person, came round to see the farm buildings, and to see if there had been any neglect on the part of the Vicar who was leaving, and to see if any repairs were necessary. We were luckier in this than many farmers, for the buildings were never allowed to get badly out of order. I remember a new roof being given to the cowshed (y beudu) (between the barn and the stables). The mason was '*mashwn mawr*' who lived down in Cwmcerrig (a big, lame, bad tempered man), and the carpenter was Jim Saer. Between them they bungled it: they either cut the beams too short or did not build the wall up far enough. You can see to this day that the roof does not run evenly from one end to the other, leaving a step between the cowshed and the stables. What was there before, I don't know. It could have been thatch. I know the timber was very rotten, and Jim Saer had to be very careful in climbing up to test and pierce the wood. Mashwn Mawr was the father of Dafi Llwyngwyn, another mason.

There was another mason – Mashwn Bach, Bancyffordd, gwr Nansi, (shop Nansi) and the uncle of Sami, the father of the people who are at Dancapel now.

We went to Capel Mair School along two ways. The usual one was across to Triolmawr, and out at Bwlchyddwyrhos, and along the road to Bancyffordd, and so down to Capel Mair. Tŷ'r Gât was occupied in those days by Daniel and Mari – and Het, Mari's mother, if I remember rightly. I attended a Cwrdd Gwylnos there as a boy of about 14. While we were singing the hymn, the donkey joined in. But read my 'Welsh Country Upbringing'. A lot of these things are in that. The donkey was kept to bring back errands and some shopping for the neighbours – and hidden under everything, a cask of beer, for Tŷ'r Gât was one of those places called a *Shebeen* (a place where beer and spirits were sold without a license). Fair play to the neighbours, the nearest pub was some miles away, and they used to turn in here in the evenings, quietly, and in small numbers, so as not to arouse suspicion. Daniel was never found out (Daniel was the roadman in that part of the parish).

Crosshans (Crosshands) was also occupied by Esther and Dafi, they once lived at Blaentriolau. Their father was the brother of John, Pantymeillion (his wife was a sister of my grandfather of Gellidywyll) and so related by marriage.

Rhospant (now in ruins) just above Bancyffordd was occupied off and on when I was in school, but generally for short periods by a squatter type of people, who had little in the way of character to lose. When empty, we would go into the garden and eat the gooseberries.

The other way of going to school was through the Cwm. It was sheltered and we went that way in drizzly weather. It was also quicker. We went down to the _allt_ at the bottom of Parc Ribyn (on the Triolmawr side), then down, turning right to cross the brook, and so on Triolmawr's side until we crossed the Shedi at Cwmllwyd. There was a house there then and a smithy. Enoc, Glynllwyd, who was originally a blacksmith, used to go down there and do all the blacksmith work that he needed. There were gooseberry bushes there too, and we used to get good feasts at the proper season.

From Cwmllwyd we followed a path that kept near the river until we came to Cwmcerrig. Then, over the bridge, past an old house called Gwargoylan, up to the road coming down from Waunmeirch, up through the allt, over near the top of the top fields of Rhydybenne, across the road to the fields of Brale farm, through Cnwcyreithin farm, and so to Capel Mair.

And now for the old roads which were used before that was made from Hewl Bancyffordd to Llanpumsaint (Rhyd Shedi) across to Pantglas, and out to St James.

The places where the roads would make to in those days were the small market towns, the turnpike road, and to the mill. This last was very important, and old roads always lead to mills and parish churches. As our road runs today, through the middle of the farms from Blaenshedi across to Cwmnant Einon, it would seem that it went above the then cultivated portions of the farms – the parts already fenced in. The parts above it were probably at that time open uplands, perhaps cultivated in small sections here and there. The tasks of subduing these top portions were undertaken as money and labour became available, and of course the need for more arable land as the stock grew. When they finally assumed the form they do today cannot now be discovered, but it would be as better ploughs became available, and the change was made from bullocks to horses. Before the present road was made and began to be used, all the farms' outlets were down to the Cwm, where there was a very old road, coming up from the Cwm beyond Blaennantrhys farm, past the farm, and out near Bwlchyddwyrhos. It then went down between Blaenshedi and Glyncoch, past Graig Icin, between Glyn Llwyd and Triolmawr down to Cwmllwyd. It can be traced for the greater part of the way to this day, though the river may have washed away its course here and there. After leaving Cwmllwyd, it began to climb the steep side of Allt Gaerwen, right up to the hedge between Gaerwen Ucha and Gaerwen Isha. It must have been very steep as it went up along this hedge, and past the old gaer on Gaerwenisha's field. Here, every trace of it is lost. It may have branched here, one branch going towards Tŷ Maen, down the cwm and up

174

the old road between Mowntan and Gilgynydd. The other branch, I should imagine, would point down towards Cwmsaer and up Penrallt farm and out to Rhengae. But one branch very probably would go somewhere towards the ford by Rhydybenne, and so down to Pentre Cwrt and the mill. All the farmers in that part of the parish called the <u>Gransh</u> had to take their grain to Felin Cwrt. The Gransh was that part of the parish situated between the rivers Shedi and Gwiddyl, but Triolbrith was in the Gransh. Whether the boundary was changed in later times to make a more workable division of the parish, I don't know, but the parish history (I believe I am right) says that it followed the Shedi from the Teifi to the ford (rhyd) at Rhydybenne, and then followed the road up past Clais and Belon, and up to the mountain. Brooks and rivers were generally boundaries that marked territorial divisions in ancient times, because they were permanent and not easily interfered with.

To return again to this old road (according to the parish history it was called <u>Hewl y Coaches</u>, because Howells, Triolmawr, once a year went along it in his carriage to keep it open for another year, and to hold the community's right to use it. He was at Triolmawr when your great grandfather was at Triolbrith. He was said to be a very kind neighbour, and when your great grandfather and great grandmother were away in the market, he would always walk across to see that all the children were safe and well.

The following may be worth telling. He was a bachelor and kept a housekeeper, <u>Hanna'r Lodge</u> who lived in her last days at the bottom house at Trolon. He was attacked and killed in Lamb Inn in a dispute, so it is surmised, over some woman. When it became known, poor Hannah had nothing but the wages that were coming to her. My grandparents felt sorry for her, and helped by taking casks of butter and things that could be carried over to Triolbrith to hide them, so that she could have something at least.

Now, as I said, all the outlets from the farms around were out to this old road – Blaennantrhys, Bwlchyddwyrhos, Blaenshedi were quite near to it. The road down from Triol-mawr to it is in good condition to this day, so is the road coming down from Glyncoch and Glynllwyd, and they can be traced to it. So also is the road going down from Gaer-wenucha. But where did the road from Triolbrith go? Well, it went down probably through Caegwair Isha (the old gap – bwlch – in the hedge where it entered Parcribin can be seen to this day). It then went down to the corner of Parcribyn. There is a canfa there today, but if you examine the rock on your left hand side after going over the canfa, you will find that it has been cut so as to give plenty of room for a cart to pass. It looks too narrow for a cart, but very probably some of the rock on the right hand side has crumbled away. Then again, remember it was for the use of the bullock carts, and they were narrower. The road, as you will notice, turns left towards the river. Where it forded the river, I don't know, but anywhere there would be possible. The road from the river up towards Gaerwen is traceable to this day. At the top it turned down towards Cwmllwyd, and into the old road.

You will have noticed the row of laburnum trees (meillion) running down the middle of Caegwair Isha. Well, father decided that he was not going to keep that bottom part again for hay, so he wired it off and allowed it to be grazed with Parcribyn. He did not mean to have a row of trees there, but he used <u>meillion</u> stakes, and, with one or two exceptions, they all took root and grew into this splendid row. I took a photograph of it, and sent it up to the <u>FIELD</u> where it appeared about thirty years ago (say 1946).

I hope you enjoy and treasure this little bit of information.

All the best, Winston,

Uncle Dan

*   *   *

October 5th, 1978

Dear Winston,
Thank you for the Parish Newsletter and your own letter that came this morning. Today is my birthday, and I am 87 years

of age. I keep thinking of my parents at that time – they were young: Father about 23, and Mother about 26. They hadn't got their feet under them then, for they had only been in the farm one year. But I know they rejoiced to see me – I was supposed to be a very beautiful infant. They were good parents and God bless all such.

Now to other matters. I want to send something for St James' Harvest Festival. It is a place very dear to me, and my parents, my brothers Jim, Johnnie, and Tommy rest there. I am sending you a cheque. Please put it in an envelope, and put it on the plate when it comes round. I hope you will have a nice service, and nice weather for it. It is wonderful to live to this age, and I can see and hear and walk about, and have no aches and pains. I keep thanking God every day,

With love,

Uncle Dan

*　　*　　*

November 1978

My dear Winston,
Christmas is coming near, and though I don't send Christmas cards now, I send greetings to all my friends that I like to

remember. So here's Blwyddyn Newydd Dda a Nadolig Llawen i ti. I often think about you and wonder what sort of work is going on, on the farm. There seemed to be a lot of ploughing done in the Autumn at one time. I don't think you do any ploughing in the Autumn now, but I'm sure there is plenty of other work to do, ready for the winter.

Well, I can't complain here. I take my daily walk – when the weather gets too cold, I shall keep inside.

With all best wishes,

Uncle Dan

*   *   *

Dec. 12th, 1978

My dear Winston,

I don't send Christmas cards, but I like to send the greetings of the season to my friends and relatives. I may have sent them in my last letter, but you are on my list and I am sending a dozen of them off these days. Can you give me Gwynoro's address? I used to call on him always at Golden Grove, and Kate and I called on him at Llanon.

There is very little news. I am keeping quite well, leading a quiet life, just reading and doing a little writing. A person came to see me today from Pontypridd because he had liked my books, and he paid a great tribute to them. He said "They made a Welshman of me." Another fellow said the other day: "I was brought up on your books," and to see great authors quoting from them – it gives one great pleasure. I must have written better than I knew.

Nadolig Llawen i chi i gyd a Blwyddyn Newydd Dda.

Nwncwl Dan

*   *   *

(Date unknown, but written after his last visit to Triolbrith, before his death)

Dear Winston,

I arrived back yesterday after a nice quiet journey, at 2 p.m. I had a marvellous time down in the country with you – and good weather to go out and see all I had long wanted to see – St James' and Capel Mair, and attend the services once again, and to see Triolbrith looking so nice with so many improvements carried out. It was nice to see the children grown up so much. I won't be so long next time.

With kind regards and all good wishes,

Uncle Dan

Uncle Dan on holiday in Gellidywyll,
when he was young.

Uncle Dan died in 1981, and the funeral service, before the cremation, was held in St Luke's Church, Newport.

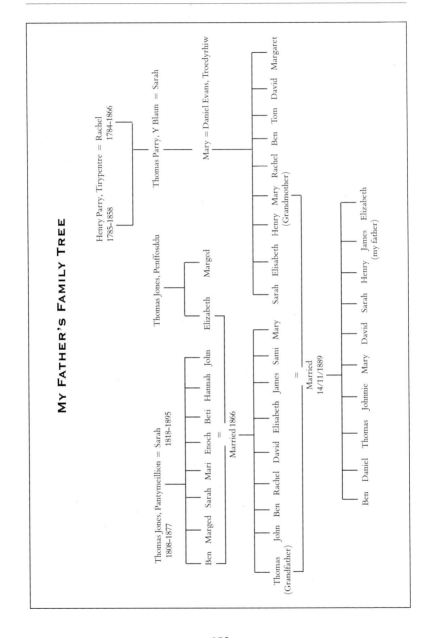

MY FATHER'S FAMILY TREE

Henry Parry, Tirypentre = Rachel
1785-1858   1784-1866

Thomas Parry, Y Blaun = Sarah

Mary = Daniel Evans, Troedyrhiw

Henry Mary Rachel Ben Tom David Margaret
(Grandmother)

Thomas Jones, Penffosddu

Elizabeth   Marged

Sarah Elisabeth

Thomas Jones, Pantymeillion = Sarah
1808-1877   1818-1895

Ben Marged Sarah Mari Enoch Beti Hannah John

=
Married 1866

Thomas John Ben Rachel David Elisabeth James Sami Mary

=
Married
14/11/1889

Thomas
(Grandfather)

Ben Daniel Thomas Johnnie Mary David Sarah Henry James Elizabeth
(my father)

182

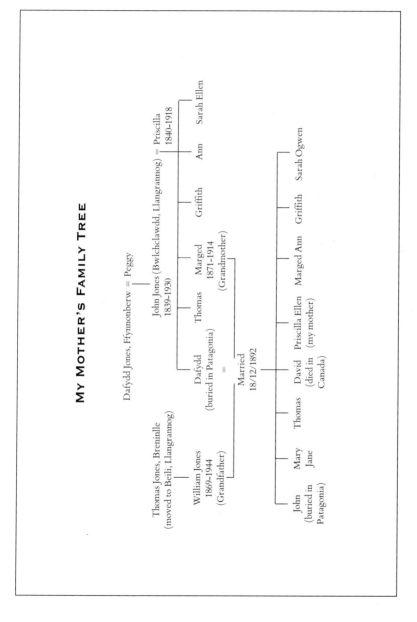

MY MOTHER'S FAMILY TREE

Dafydd Jones, Ffynnonberw = Peggy

Thomas Jones, Breninlle
(moved to Beili, Llangrannog)

John Jones (Bwlchclawdd, Llangrannog) = Priscilla
1839-1930   1840-1918

William Jones
1869-1944
(Grandfather)

Dafydd
(buried in Patagonia)
=
Married
18/12/1892

Thomas   Marged   Griffith   Ann   Sarah Ellen
         1871-1914
         (Grandmother)

John   Mary   Thomas   David   Priscilla Ellen   Marged Ann   Griffith   Sarah Ogwen
(buried in Jane   (died in   (my mother)
Patagonia)   Canada)

183